let's talk

let's talk

One-on-One, Peer, and Small-Group Writing Conferences

Mark Overmeyer

Stenhouse Publishers
Portland, Maine

Stenhouse Publishers
www.stenhouse.com

Library of Congress Cataloging-in-Publication Data Pending
Overmeyer, Mark
  Let's Talk
ISBN 978-1-57110-855-5 (pbk.: alk. paper) ISBN 978-1-62531-046-0 (ebook)

Cover and interior design by Lucian Burg, Lu Design Studios, Portland, ME
www.ludesignstudios.com

Manufactured in the United States of America

PRINTED ON 30% PCW
   RECYCLED PAPER

21 20 19 18 17 16 15   9 8 7 6 5 4 3 2 1

Dedicated to the many students and teachers
who have taught me so much about writing
for the past thirty years

CONTENTS

ACKNOWLEDGMENTS

I could not write a book without the support of teachers who have opened their classrooms to me over the years. Thank you to Principal Marj McDonald and the teachers at Sandburg Elementary in Littleton for supporting the chapter on peer conferences. To Sharon Miller at Franklin Elementary: your students are so lucky. Years ago I witnessed truly independent peer conferences in your second-grade classroom, and your success has inspired me ever since to think of what students can do on their own. Thank you, Jan DiSanti, Carrie Palmer, Katrina Shroyer, and Beth O'Loughlin, for all your support at Eastridge Elementary. Beth, you make me a better teacher when you push me to think of how best to support English language learners. You also help me remember the strengths language learners bring to our classrooms.

I remember all of the energy I felt every time I walked into Barb Minoegue's fifth-grade classroom at Fox Hollow Elementary to learn more about how talk can support students' writing. Barb, your welcoming classroom environment made me feel at home from day one of this project.

So many professional writers have served as mentors while writing this book. Thank you to Carl Anderson, Jeff Anderson, Cris Tovani, Katie Wood Ray, Kelly Gallagher, Penny Kittle, Patrick Allen, and Donalyn Miller. Your writing inspires me every time I sit down with my journal. I could not do this kind of work without mentors like you.

let's talk

At Stenhouse: Thank you, Bill Varner, for being an editor, a poet, and a friend. Chandra Lowe, you are the best dinner companion ever, and I look forward to seeing you at future conferences. Zsofi McMullin, thank you for keeping me on my toes with my blog and my Twitter posts . . . I know I have a long way to go. Chris Downey, thank you for all the work you do to help manuscripts make their way to publication.

Thank you, Dennis, for understanding when I need to write. It is difficult to find time away from our busy lives, and this book would never have happened without your support and encouragement.

Why Talk?

It was May, toward the end of the school year, and when I walked in to visit Jan Disanti's class, the students knew why I was there: to talk about writing.

"How are you guys doing? How is your writing going?"

VaShaun told me he was writing about how important his grandmother was in his life, but when I sat down next to him, he paged all the way back to a story he had first worked on last September (Figure 1).

"You know what I want to talk to you about," he said. "The goat."

"You still have more to say about the goat?" I asked.

"You know I do."

VaShaun loves to tell stories, but he is rarely interested in writing his stories down. For months now, he had been telling and retelling his story of slapping a charging goat in a petting zoo. Every time he reached the punch line: "And then I reached back and *slapped* that goat upside the head!" the class would roar with laughter and ask him to tell the story again. Sometimes they would challenge him in a friendly way: "Wait a minute, VaShaun. Did you *really* slap the goat?" VaShaun did not enter Jan's writing class as a willing participant. He resisted writing, even though he received so much attention for his stories.

VaShaun gained confidence as a writer in Jan's class because of talk. The talk began with VaShaun telling the story, continued as his peers responded positively, and culminated with encouraging words from his teachers. The energy to write began with talk, the first draft resulted from talk, and the revisions continued because of talk.

1

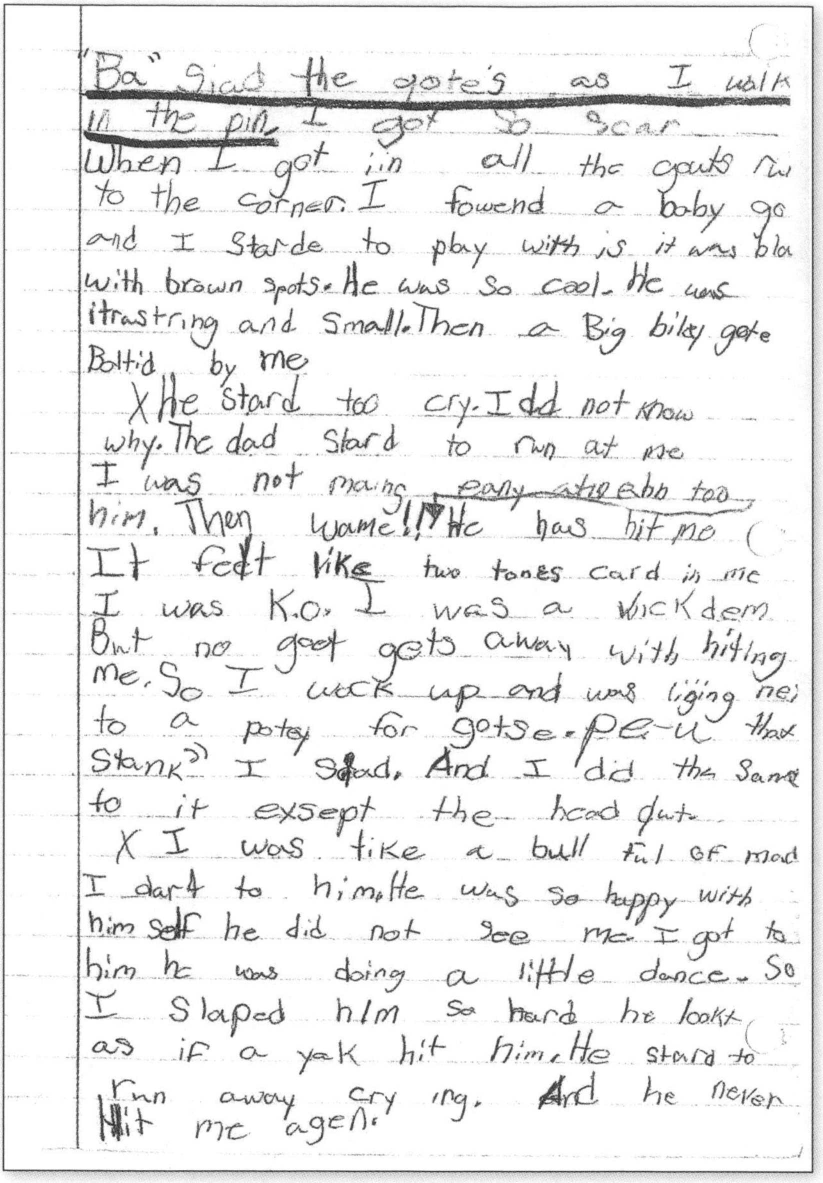
"Ba" siad the gote's as I walk
in the pin I got so scar
When I got iin all the gauts ru
to the corner. I fowend a baby go
and I starde to play with is it was bla
with brown spots. He was so cool. He was
itrastring and small. Then a Big biky gote
Boltid by me
X He stard too cry. I dd not know
why. The dad stard to run at me
I was not maing eany atreabo too
him. Then wame!! He has hit me
It feet like two tones card in me
I was K.O. I was a wickdem
But no goot gets away with hiting
me. So I wock up and was liging nei
to a potey for gotse. "Pe-u that
stank" I siad. And I did the same
to it exsept the head out.
X I was like a bull ful of mad
I dart to him. He was so happy with
him self he did not see me. I got to
him he was doing a little dance. So
I slaped him so hard he lookt
as if a yak hit him. He stard to
run away cry ing. And he never
hit me agen.

Figure 1 VaShaun's writing draft

When VaShaun called me over, he wanted to hear me laugh one more time when I read the piece, but he also wanted some advice.

"Can you help me make my writing better?" he asked.

I spent a moment reading over his latest draft.

"VaShaun, you make such a clear picture in my mind in this part of your writing when you describe the goat after he butted into you: 'I dart to him. When I got to him he was doing a little dance.' I am wondering if you could pick another spot in your story and stretch it out in the same way you did here. The picture in my mind of that dancing goat just won't go away."

Within a few minutes, VaShaun, who a few months before would rarely write, much less revise, found a spot where he could add a picture in the reader's mind right after the goat butted him (Figure 2):

> It felt like two ton whales flopped on me. I thought I was dead. I saw the light. But then I started to come back little by little . . .

Figure 2 VaShaun works on creating a picture in the reader's mind.

VaShaun was willing to revise his writing and take new risks because he did not see me as his evaluator. He trusted me because I cared about his stories, cared about his writing, and spent time pointing out his strengths. Trusting relationships in a writing classroom can only be built through meaningful talk.

When he independently strengthened his writing, VaShaun demonstrated his growth as a writer. He is now the kind of writer who understands the craft of writing these types of stories (slow down at the most interesting moments) and the process of writing (pick one part you like and try to make it better—do not rewrite the entire story). Conferences with teachers and talks with peers supported VaShaun more effectively than a rubric or written responses on his work. He is not the kind of writer who pays much attention to what is written on his papers, but he is the type of writer who routinely gives himself the highest scores on a rubric. While I am not suggesting that rubrics and self-evaluation have no merit, I do believe that rubrics have not solved all the issues surrounding feedback for developing writers. Comments derived only from the language of a rubric do not ring "true" to students, and the most authentic way to be real, or "true," is to enter into a conversation with the writer about his writing.

The Benefits of Conferring

The value of conferring with students in the writing workshop is well documented. In his seminal work *Writing: Teachers and Children at Work*, Donald Graves reminds us of the importance of conferring: "The teacher looks for a child's potential in the words used in a conference . . . rather than becoming anxious about the final product, the teacher who looks for potential sees possibility in a shard of information" (1984, 100). Graves's words of advice are perhaps more important now than when he wrote them thirty years ago. In the age of standards, if we keep our minds too laser focused only on students meeting grade-level expectations, we may forget to look for possibilities. While we can certainly gather important information from writing conferences, all of the information does not have to be pigeonholed inside of a predetermined standard. Talking with our students can do so much more than provide assessment data. Talking can help us build relationships.

In *How's It Going?*, Carl Anderson recommends a conversational tone during conferences. The title suggests a friendly, open-ended dialogue when meeting with students one-on-one. It doesn't mean that Anderson believes clear teaching cannot happen during conferences. He warns us to not be "mesmerized by what students are writing about because the goal of the conference is to teach the writer something" (2000, 8). So, even if we are fascinated by the topic of a student's piece (think of VaShaun's goat story), or if we have a personal connection with the topic, we do not need to share our observations or connections at length. Otherwise, we lose the point of why we engage in a conference. It is a teaching and learning place, not just a sharing place.

One of the best ways to help students build confidence is through the types of conversations Anderson describes. Without talk, students cannot develop a sense of being a writer or of living a writerly life. In *Choice Words*, Peter Johnston describes this as developing a narrative: "To solve the many problems I will encounter as a writer, and to persist through the many revisions I will face, I have to weave myself into a narrative in which I am the kind of person who encounters and solves problems with text. I develop this belief through a history of conversation with others around my writing" (2004, 30).

VaShaun had many conversations about his writing, and he was therefore becoming part of a narrative in which he was a writer. That's why he had so much confidence when I approached him at the end of the year. All he had to say was, "You know what I want to talk about." This was his way of inviting me into a continued dialogue.

Rethinking Talk

I share VaShaun's story at the beginning of this book as an example of how even short conferences can be powerful tools for guiding our students' writing. Intentional talk is a powerful tool for increasing student achievement and motivation. Talk transformed VaShaun from a resister to a writer.

In the writing workshop, talking has many benefits, which I have experienced as both a teacher and a learner:

1. **Students' interests and backgrounds as writers emerge when we talk in the workshop.** When we talk with our students about their writing, and when they talk with one another, we learn far beyond what is on the page. We can learn concrete information, such as what students like to do outside of school, and we can also learn about how much they know about themselves as writers. For example, a student may tell us he likes to play football after school, and he has been on the same winning team for two years. But he may also reveal that he doesn't know how to write about his ideas because he can't quite put his thoughts on the page.

2. **Talk provides the opportunity for all writers to reflect on their own writing progress.** When students talk with teachers and one another about their writing, they can use this talk to internalize their own knowledge and progress. Even when the entire class is providing feedback to a student about the poem she wrote for her grandmother, all writers in the room can think about how those strategies can support their own growth as writers. Through engaged conversations, all work becomes more contextualized.

3. **Talk provides an opportunity to build a community of writers who rely on one another, not just on the teacher, for advice, affirmation, and support.** One possible disadvantage to one-on-one conferences might be that students come to rely on the teacher as the only source of support for writing. In fact, every writer in the room—students and the teacher—can provide support. If we provide students with opportunities to work with peers, they can talk with one another while a teacher is talking with one student or a small group of students.

4. **Talk will help to teach students the language of writing.** All of our ideas must live in language first before we transfer them to writing. Frequent, intentional talk about writing products and processes will help all learners to become stronger writers. When we talk with our entire class during a mini-lesson about generating ideas, we are teaching them the language of writing in the same way we are teaching an individual student about the language of writing during a one-on-one conference. Intentional talk about the writing process is important for all learners, but it is essential for English language learners. Throughout this book, I will provide suggestions in various sections about how to engage ELLs through talk in the writing workshop.

Structuring Talk in the Writing Workshop

Individual conferences increase talk in the writing workshop, but if we insist on viewing a conference as only a one-on-one, single-student-at-a-time experience, we may never feel comfortable as writing teachers. We feel guilty when we do not meet with every student each week, we feel incompetent when we aren't sure what to say to a student, and even when we emerge from an effective conference with a student, we wonder whether we spent too much time with one student while ignoring the needs of the class.

If the purpose of a conference is to learn about and guide writers, and if we know that talk can move writers in powerful ways, perhaps we need to broaden our perspective about conferences in the writing workshop. We can structure talk in the workshop in a variety of ways.

In this book, I will provide ideas for how to organize and manage the "classic" one-on-one conference, but I will also offer alternative structures that can help students grow as writers.

These structures will be categorized by the type of talk that might occur in the writing workshop for various purposes and at various times—talks between teachers and students and talks between students and their peers.

If we think back to VaShaun for a moment, here are the ways he could grow as a writer through talk:

1. He could meet with his teacher in a **one-on-one conference**.
2. He could become a member of a teacher-led **small-group conference**.
3. He could reflect on his writing with the teacher during a **teacher-led public conference**.
4. He could talk with one of his classmates during a **peer conference**.
5. He could meet with a small group of classmates during a **peer review conference**.

These structures are offered as possibilities for your work as a teacher of writing. Ultimately, we all want our writers to improve. The more "talk structures" we introduce to our students, the more likely we are to meet their diverse needs. Students may begin to request a particular kind of talk in the writing classroom rather than waiting to meet with the designated "teacher." If I view a conference as a single story line involving only one teacher and one student, then I limit other ways talk can benefit the writing workshop.

As VaShaun taught me over the course of a few months, there is more than one way to tell a tale. His story about a goat's comeuppance is one I will never forget.

Though I cannot match his storytelling ability, I view my role in this book as a teacher relating stories of working in real classrooms with real writers, hoping to share what I learned along the way.

PART 1

Teacher-Student Talk

CHAPTER 1

Qualities of Effective Feedback

I once heard Kathy Collins, an author and staff developer at Teachers College, Columbia University, speak about the "Oh no you didn't!" stories we all have as teachers.

The story that immediately popped into my head had to do with feedback and what *not* to do as a writing teacher.

When I was getting my master of arts in the teaching of writing, I was frustrated when I had to rewrite my thesis for the third time. I showed the thesis to my fifth graders, page by page, and complained about how hard it was to write. I said things like: "I know you think all I do is sit at home and come up with assignments for you. Well, I am in school too. You think you have homework! Look at this! I have to redo this entire thirty-page paper! My professor only liked one page, so I have to start over!"

I then proceeded to teach writing.

Needless to say, students did not exactly enjoy writing that day, and neither did I.

Breaking this incident down a bit, I was giving feedback to the group. The feedback was about how frustrating writing is and how much I didn't like it. When I look back, I see the irony: I complained to fifth graders about writing my thesis, and my topic was engaging students in the writing workshop.

It turns out that complaining about writing does not engage students!

Feedback begins the moment the workshop starts: how we feel about writing is clear to our students every day. One of my favorite video clips of workshop instruction begins with a teacher saying to his students, "Writers, I read your writing last night, and I'm so excited."

This teacher is on to something: the idea that it is exciting to read student work. His students can now picture their teacher on the couch, reading their writing, laughing during the funny parts, thinking about his students' lives while at home—perhaps no more powerful feedback can ever be given.

We must let our students know that writing, and reading their writing, is both a powerful and a joyful act.

Effective Feedback

We know a lot about what makes feedback effective and ineffective, but as John Hattie (2011) points out in *Visible Learning for Teachers,* there are many variables to consider. Let's look at Hattie's categories for kinds of feedback and then dig a bit deeper into what makes feedback effective.

Hattie recommends we consider feedback as a series of questions first: Where am I going? How am I going there? Where to next?

Where Am I Going?

When we provide feedback to students during a writing workshop, it does not occur in a vacuum. Students should know the goals of our lessons and units of study. Then, our feedback can be based on these goals.

This does not mean that there is no choice in the workshop or that we only give feedback based in the narrow lens of what we have just taught. But keeping in mind the goal for the day (e.g., strengthening leads to a story) or the unit (e.g., developing a review of a favorite book) helps contextualize our feedback so that it is more meaningful for students. If we are too broad and comment on just anything we notice in student writing, we confuse them. If we are too narrow and focus only on recently taught material, we might give the impression that writing is compartmentalized and exists only in the small world of our classrooms. They may come away from continual, narrowly focused conferences believing the purpose of writing is to please us.

Our thinking about where we are going with students may vary depending on the time of year. In the beginning of the year, for example, I may spend a fair amount of time just getting to know my students as writers. But I can still connect this to a clear purpose by letting students know that I am going to learn about them by asking questions about their writing lives. These kinds of questions can help teachers get to know their writers:

"How did you come up with this idea?"
"Why did you change that part?"
"Tell me more about _____."
"When you get stuck, what do you normally do?"

Once we establish that writing should be based on a clear vision of where we are going, we can think about how students get there.

How Am I Going There?

Once students are writing, they need feedback about how they are doing along the way. This is where feedback becomes both the trickiest and the most powerful. Grant Wiggins (2012), in his article "Seven Keys to Effective Feedback," provides some advice for us about how to make sure we make the most of feedback once the work has begun. We will examine a few of these here.

Goal referenced

When conferences with individual students are based on specific goals, they are more meaningful. For example, if I base my conference on some of my goals as a teacher (getting to know students, supporting students through their processes), then, when I enter into a conference, I can name the goal for students so that I can become transparent (another one of Wiggins's seven keys). I might say the following:

"My goal is to just get to know you better as a writer. Can we just talk for a bit about your writer's notebook and you can speak to how you developed your ideas?"

"My goal is to help you become a more efficient writer. When we last
talked, you shared that you sometimes get stuck, not knowing
how to start even when you have an idea. Can we just talk about
that for a bit, and then we'll see if I can give you some tips?"

When students set the stage by sharing what they want to talk
about, the feedback is automatically meaningful because you are
working from their lead. When I worry a student will not accept my
feedback, or when I realize I am talking too much and not listening
to the student, I ask them to set a goal. I might say, "Let's set a goal
right now about what you might do with your writing. What are you
thinking about?" If they do not respond, I may offer choices so that
we can set a goal together: "Do you want to focus on word choice,
or maybe the lead? How about that one part where we thought you
might add another scene?" I try to let the writer take as much of the
lead as possible while goal-setting for feedback because then I know
the feedback is more likely to pay off. If they set the goal completely
on their own, or with my support, then the buy-in is more likely.

Actionable

When we comment on students' writing, whether verbally or in written
comments, we need to make sure our comments create a possibility for
current or future action. Comments such as "Good job" or "Awesome!"
or rubric scores are not actionable. We may think we are building
students' confidence with positive praise such as "Great job!" but in
reality, as Carol Dweck (2006) in her influential book *Mindset* points
out, we are not supporting their growth. There are a few problems with
generic praise. When we say to a student, "You are such a good writer!"
we might do the following:

- Take agency away from the students, making them dependent
  on our praise.
- Confuse students by focusing comments on what we think
  without connecting it to any kind of future work. What
  if a student has no idea why we think a piece of writing is
  "awesome"? How can they replicate this kind of work?

- Create an atmosphere where all students start to expect us to tell them if their writing is good, when in reality we want our students to internalize strong writing for themselves. Of course, we need to teach them what quality work looks like, but we need to help them internalize these qualities so they don't depend on us for affirmation all the time.

Actionable feedback, whether from a teacher or from a peer, should support writers with specificity and no judgment. For example, instead of pointing to a stronger portion of student writing and saying, "Wow! This is awesome! Can you do something like this in this other part of your paper?" more effective feedback might sound like this: "Right here, you made a picture in my mind of the beach that day. I can see it and almost feel what it was like. I am wondering if you can add the same kind of details here where it is harder to picture what happens when you go in the ocean."

Wiggins (2012) also recommends that feedback be manageable. We do not want to overwhelm a student with feedback. It takes knowledge of a student to know how much may be too much, but in general, my rule of thumb is to give one piece of praise ("Right here, as a writer, you _____") and one piece of advice ("Right here, I wonder if you could _____" or "You might _____"). I know some students who can handle multiple pieces of advice, and I would certainly leave that up to your expertise as a teacher who works with students every day. There is no one "rule" about how to make feedback actionable, but if students do not act on it, then it is likely that you were either not clear or the student was overwhelmed.

Timely feedback

Feedback is most effective when students have the opportunity to change what they are doing during the drafting stages.

No matter how long I teach, this scenario happens: I have not met with a particular writer for a while, and when I finally sit down to read over a piece, it is long and unwieldy. But the writer is sitting in front of me, smiling, waiting to hear about how great I think the piece is. It is hard not to notice the errors in both larger-order concerns, such as meaning and organization, and smaller-order concerns, such as grammar and mechanics.

I have three choices as a teacher of writing:

1. Pick one or two things to talk to the writer about.
2. "Bank" the knowledge I now have for this student and just wait until another opportunity to work with the writing earlier in the process.
3. Ask the student to work with me on most everything I noticed that is wrong.

I used to take the third option. I would often ask the student to come in at lunch so that we could "fix" the writing together. But now I see why that is not the most effective strategy for the writer, for the writing, or for me.

The train has left the station if a student has many pages of completed writing and you have a difficult time deciphering the purpose or you are dismayed by the number of errors. We need to meet with these students before they've written so much that fixing the writing is frustrating. Don't feel guilty if this happens. Sometimes, early in the year, you don't know the students who need you first. Even when you know this, life gets busy. But don't forget the rule of timeliness when you are trying to figure out whether to give feedback. You don't want to teach students that writing is frustrating. Even as an adult, the frustrating experience of having the thirty-page draft of my master's thesis rejected still haunts me. I should have sought help long before the thirty pages, but I didn't. My professor didn't have any choice. I basically needed to start again.

But as a teacher, you do have a choice. You can teach the student that you care about the writing by focusing on one or two things to praise, and then you may cue some focused revisions or edits. Or, you may simply say to the student: "Tell me how I can support you with this piece. What would you like to talk about?" or "The next time you begin writing a piece, I want to talk to you earlier in the process.

You have done so much work here, but I am thinking I can provide better advice when you are working on your next draft. What are you thinking?" This second option teaches students you care about them as writers. This allows you to acknowledge their work, and you also commit to meeting with them earlier the next time.

Ongoing

Once we know our writers, we can provide new feedback in the context of previous feedback. This is my favorite part of conferences: when we know writers so well that we can talk about growth or previous pieces they have written. Nothing builds identity for a writer more effectively than the ability to converse about previous writing: "This lead reminds me of that lead you wrote in the story about your new cat. You wrote it after we studied leads as a class, remember?" "Remember before when you told me you didn't like to write at all? Now look at your notebook! Look how many pages you have written. What do you think made the difference for you?"

Written or verbal feedback?

For the purposes of this book, verbal feedback will be the primary focus. Feedback can be written as well. There isn't necessarily one form of feedback that is better than another, though I would argue that the power of sitting down with a writer side by side is difficult to replicate when contrasted with commenting directly on the document. If written feedback is used, then perhaps this question can guide its effectiveness: Does the written feedback you provide help students to become stronger, more enthusiastic, and more effective writers? If the answer is "yes," then the written feedback is probably working.

It isn't a matter of whether we should provide written feedback. Rather, it is a matter of effectiveness. The result should be that students internalize the feedback to become stronger writers. If you give written feedback, here are a few tips:

- Keep it short.
- Focus on a few items to praise by naming what is working. Just

as in verbal feedback, as Dweck (2006) reminds us, avoid words such as "awesome" or "great."

- Cue students to revise or edit only a few items. Avoid doing the editing for them. Students should become stronger at revising and editing their own work. If you "fix" their errors for them, then you are becoming their technical editor rather than their teacher.

- Do not give written feedback to students if they do not respond to it positively. It is too much work, and you are likely to get more accomplished in a short conversation.

Where to Next?

Once we have offered feedback to students regarding their drafts, we can think with them about what is next. This is where knowledge of a student is key. We need to figure out what kind of challenge would help them grow as writers. Hattie (2011) points out that feedback is most effective when students have not yet mastered something. If students already know how to do something, then they don't need our feedback to keep on this same course. They may just need more time.

This "where to next?" question is a component of longer-term goal setting. During conferences, we provide tips and cues, and then we check up on our students to see how their work is progressing. But when we think of next steps, we can help them to make longer-term goals, challenging them to move beyond where they are today. We might ask the following questions:

"What kind of work would you like to try as a writer while we work on this unit?"

"Can you think of a writer who can be a mentor for you as you continue? I wonder if you can find a mentor text and learn some strategies from someone who has already done this work."

"Since you already feel comfortable with _____, let's think of something that would push you as a writer so that you can get even stronger."

Getting Better at Feedback

The only way to get better at feedback is the same way we get better at anything: practice.

If I want to know whether my feedback is effective, I have learned to ask the students directly. I ask them to talk about how the feedback worked and what might have made it better. I might ask the following:

> "We talked yesterday about _____. How did it go for you when you worked on your story some more? Did the feedback help you? How?"
>
> "Remember you said I could write a few ideas on your piece to help you with how to _____? Did the comments help? How?"

Just as we need to give our students timely feedback, we also need to know the results of our feedback. If I talk with a student about a piece of writing, I must touch base with the student at the end of class or during the next class period. I want to make sure they know I am checking on how the work we talked about is paying off. If I wait too long, they may not become stronger writers, and I may lose an opportunity to see whether my own feedback work is helping them. Timeliness cuts both ways.

CHAPTER 2

One Teacher, One Student: The "Classic" Conference

One teacher and one student. This is the kind of structure most of us probably envision when we think of writing conferences. A one-on-one conference is useful during all stages of the writing process. As students plan, draft, revise, edit, and prepare their pieces for publication, they can benefit from conversations with a teacher about their progress. We can confer with individual students in the beginning of the year or the beginning of a unit when we just want to get to know our students as people and as writers. If this is our purpose—to know our writers—then a conference should truly be a conversation. As soon as we move into the realm of teaching, writing conferences become more difficult because we are advising our students, and this is when the impact of feedback must be carefully examined.

Feedback

Conferences are a tricky business, as noted in Chapter 1, because feedback is tricky. As John Hattie notes in his book on research-based teaching practices, *Visible Learning for Teachers*, "Feedback is among the most common features of successful teaching and learning. But there is an enigma: while feedback is among the most powerful moderators of learning, its effects are among the most variable" (2011, 115).

Feedback has varied results on student achievement because teachers cannot control how students respond to it. Feedback is given but also received, and there's the rub. Many of us have stories of receiving cryptic feedback on our papers when we were in high school and college. The most confusing note for me, often written in red ink, read "passive verb construction." I never bothered to respond to this written feedback because I generally received As and Bs in writing.

Then, in graduate school, an English professor pulled me aside and, during a one-on-one conference, asked whether I knew what she meant by passive verb construction. I confessed I did not. She underlined a sentence with passive verbs in my paper and showed me how to write with a more active voice by eliminating the helping (to be) verbs. A five-minute conversation solved the mystery of all those comments. I still struggle with passive construction, but now I frequently spot my errors and revise my own writing.

Let's look at this story in terms of feedback: I received feedback, but I did nothing about it. I take part of the blame for this, but I think teachers play a role here as well. One five-minute conversation helped me change course. Perhaps another writer would have asked a teacher to explain the difference between active and passive voice the first time a note appeared on a paper, but for whatever reason, I did not. Feedback is ineffective if the student does not react to it.

As teachers of writing, one goal must be how to make our feedback stick. There are many ways to increase the likelihood our feedback will be relevant. As discussed in more detail in Chapter 1, we can build trusting relationships with our students, clearly set goals with student input, provide timely and relevant feedback, and ask our writers to first identify the kind of support they need. But the best advice to anyone trying to get better at feedback in a one-on-one conference is to just dig in and try it.

Sometimes, conferences go smoothly. You listen first, you give a bit of advice, you help a student set a goal, and then the goal is met. But sometimes, especially in our first attempts, conferences are not easy at all. My journey with conferences began more than twenty years ago, and I am still working on becoming a better listener, a better mentor, a better teacher. Let's consider some of the questions I am frequently asked about conferences in the writing workshop.

What Do We Talk About?

When I first began conferring, I didn't know what to say. I never ran out of ideas for leading the talk in the reading workshop, and I never worried about what to listen for when I sat in on literature circles over the years. But a writing conference is different. While it is true that students can technically be "wrong" about something offered up in a literature circle, there are respectful ways to ask for clarification. We can ask students to go back to the text, to reread, to listen to others' ideas, or to restate their ideas in a different way. But since the text in a writing conference is generated by a student, issues of ownership arise that do not come up during reading conferences.

An initial question I often ask a student of any age is quite simple: "What is your piece about?" or "What are you writing about today?" This works as an entry point for getting to know your writers because they get a chance to talk and clarify before you offer advice. Recently, I asked Neveah, a kindergarten student, to tell me about her picture.

"Hi, Neveah! What are you writing about today?"

"When I woke up and saw the moon."

Neveah's picture was a bit hard to decipher. It looked like a series of horizontal, oval-shaped scribbles. I asked her to tell me about the picture in a bit more detail. I pointed to the oval shapes in the middle of the page.

"Tell me about this part."

"It's my bed."

"Where are you? Where is the moon?"

Neveah quickly picked up a pencil to finish drawing herself (a long, vertical oval atop the horizontal ovals) and then chose a yellow crayon to draw a circle to represent the moon. All I did was ask for clarification by asking her about her story first. I didn't say, "Don't scribble," and I didn't guess at what her story was about based on the picture. I merely followed her lead. This was the end of the conference because she had met the goal (set forth in the mini-lesson) of making sure that when we write, everything on the page has to make sense.

In an intermediate classroom, after reading fourth grader Annika's description of getting ready to go on a long drive to Minnesota, I asked the same question:

"What would you say your piece is about?"

"My trip to Minnesota."

"Right now, when I read your piece, I see this description of how tired you are because you have to wake up at four in the morning, and I can tell you are dreading the long drive."

"It's about getting ready to go."

"Getting ready to go on the trip instead of the trip itself? Do you plan to write about Minnesota in this piece?"

"No. I just want to talk about the part of getting ready."

In this conference, I clarified with Annika her intended purpose. I did not tell her to change her focus, and when she clarified her intentions by responding to the simple question, "What is your piece about?" I could then see her writing had met her intentions. When writing does not match a writer's stated purpose, I can provide feedback to help them meet their goals rather than mine.

So, what about when a conference does not go quite as smoothly as the ones I just described? No matter how careful we are, sometimes students may feel judged by our feedback.

Once, after listening to a kindergarten student share her writing, I asked whether I could show what her story would look like if it were written in a book. She nodded, and I printed her words correctly on sticky notes and placed them under her writing. This technique has worked for me many times before, but in this classroom, on this particular day, she said, "Oh, I wrote it wrong," and my heart broke a little. I was supposed to be encouraging this writer, noticing what she did well, praising her for her effort and her accomplishment. And she interpreted my offer as an indication that she was "wrong." Even though I had used this same language effectively with other kindergarten students, this time, it not only didn't work, but it may have actually damaged this student's confidence.

Even after years of experience, we still may not know what to say, but I can promise you that your words will become easier the more you practice. Here are some possible sentence starters to begin conferences, based on when you might meet with students during the writing process:

In General

"How can I support you as a writer?"

"What are you working on today as a writer?"

"How is your writing going today?"

Planning Stage

Possible teacher cues:

"What are you planning to write about today?"

"Tell me about your plan."

"As a writer, what ideas do you have today?"

"I heard you talking with _____ about your writing. I cannot wait to read it. What are your plans as you think about how to begin?"

Drafting Stage

"How is your piece coming along?"

"When we talked last time, we were thinking about _____. How is that working for you as you draft this piece?"

"You seem to be moving along with this piece. How can I help you? What would you like me to listen for as you read your piece today?"

"What is one goal you have as a writer while you continue with your piece?"

"How is this piece working for you as a writer compared to the last piece you wrote?"

Revising

"How have you worked to make your writing better?"

"Can you read me some 'before and after' examples from your piece, showing me how you worked to make your writing stronger?"

"What do you do as a writer while you revise? Do you like to write the entire piece first, and then go back, or do you revise as you write?"

Preparing for Publication

"Do you have everything you need to publish your piece? What do you need from me?"

"Who is your audience for publishing your piece?"

"When you go back to edit your work, what helps you the most?"

"When I read your piece today, what would you like me to pay attention to?"

What Do I Teach?

I used to believe my conferences with students were failures if one, magical teaching point did not surface, and I cannot count how many times teachers have asked me, "What would you say to the student in this case?" or "How would you start this conference?"

I am quite happy to engage in these discussions, but I realize now that when a dialogue between a teacher and student occurs, we often do not know exactly why we say certain things. A dialogue can only be planned so far in advance. What you say in return is obviously influenced by what the student first says to you.

And yet I understand completely the discomfort of the ambiguity inherent in conferences.

The main rule of thumb I follow now is to let student writing guide me as I consider what to teach. I worry less about finding the "perfect" teaching point than first finding something sincerely honest to point out about a student strength that is evident in the writing. Then, I can move toward finding something to teach. My default teaching points are now aligned with what I teach students during the mini-lesson. Cris Tovani, a high school reading specialist and also my mentor and friend, describes this kind of conference in her article "Feedback Is a Two-Way Street":

> One way to start a conference is to ask, "How are you doing with the learning target today?" Following the vocabulary strategies mini-lesson, I sought more specific feedback by saying, "What words are throwing you off? What questions have you asked to isolate your confusion?"

> Such conversations hold students accountable for practicing and demonstrating that they can do what I've modeled. If students have mastered the target, I teach them something new. If they're struggling with the target, I give them more support. I also use conference feedback to establish small groups for students to work on their specific needs. (2012, 51)

Cris is describing formative assessment here: she is teaching, providing time for practice, and checking for understanding so that she knows what to adjust. Cris takes a learning stance first, which allows her to move beyond error hunting. She is checking to see whether her instruction has paid off.

As we confer with writers, if we seek to learn first, we will know so much better what to teach because we are actually anticipating we might need to change direction. Note that Cris does not move on if a student has not met the learning target. She decides to teach students who are meeting the target something new. My experience with writers is that sometimes the "new" may be more time to keep writing, trying out new strategies for success. In other words, sometimes my best tip for teaching writing if things are going well for a particular student is to leave them alone and let them keep writing. I actually had a first grader interrupt me during a conference when I was about to give him some advice. He said, "I thought I was supposed to write. Can I just keep writing?"

A six-year-old grounded me in one of the most important truths of writing workshop. More than anything, to get better, students need time to write. I told this student I would check in with him later after he had an opportunity to continue his story.

How Can I Find Time to Confer One on One with All My Students?

Time. It's what we all want more of, and yet it is something we can't create. We are held to a structure out of our control. We can't increase the time in the school day, and we cannot add days to the year to get conferences in—and I do not think students would appreciate teachers keeping them in from recess or lunch to hold conferences.

As I stated in the introduction, one way to view conferences in the writing workshop is to broaden our vision of conferences in the first place. I prefer to think of the many ways to structure talk rather than relying solely on one-on-one conferences. That being said, there are many benefits to meeting with students individually, so we must tackle the issue of time.

We can be flexible with the time we have. One of the uncomfortable truths about teaching is that some of our students may need more time than others. If I parse out the conferences into equal, five-minute slots for each student, and my workshop time between a mini-lesson and sharing is forty minutes, then the maximum number of conferences I can accomplish in one writing workshop is eight. This is hardly realistic because between conferences teachers may need to redirect some students or meet with others who are truly stuck. Even with a workshop that goes perfectly, if I have twenty-five to thirty students, then I will sit with my students individually every three to five days, assuming there are no interruptions, such as assemblies or fire drills.

However, we can save and shave time. We can structure our classrooms physically to allow access to more students, and we can establish routines that allow for regular conferences. Here are some tips that may save time and allow for more opportunities to meet with students individually.

> ⊃**Tip:** Differentiate clearly in your mind when you are checking in versus holding a full conference. For example, following a mini-lesson, you may decide to check in with as many students as possible just to assess their writing based on what you just taught. Focusing on the mini-lesson topic will save time. Move on if things are going well, and pause briefly to redirect if some students are confused. If many students are confused after a mini-lesson, do not hesitate to call everyone back to the meeting area to reteach a strategy or skill. It is important to their success as writers.

⊃*Tip:* Read student work in advance. This will allow you to consider some teaching points before conferences. You will already have some indication before you begin the conference about strengths and needs. Reading in advance is particularly helpful when students are writing longer pieces.

⊃*Tip:* Ask students to explain in writing *why* they want you to read their pieces. Let them "own" the conference topic. As you read, you will not only read for a specific purpose, you will know what to ask the student and find a teaching point more quickly.

⊃*Tip:* Hold your conferences in the middle of the classroom rather than on the edge of the room at a separate table. As students return to their seats to write after the conference, keep the more reluctant writers close by so that you can check in with them frequently, in between conferences. I typically do not meet at a separate table at all during conferences. I just pull up a chair or kneel by students' desks while we talk.

⊃*Tip:* Think of all interactions with an individual as a conference. While you walk around the room and help everyone get started, chat informally but specifically with your students, noticing how they are doing while they plan, draft, revise, and edit their pieces.

⊃*Tip:* Spend more intentional time up front during the planning or early drafting stages so that conferences can be more efficient later. A good start will save you time. Try to avoid situations in which students will have "finished" writing multiple pages before you have had a chance to read. It is much easier to help students navigate meaning in their early drafts.

> ⊃ *Tip:* Listen for conference topics during mini-lesson "turn and talks." Eavesdrop. Take notes. If you notice that some students are unclear about their intentions as writers, intervene by conferring with them soon after writing time begins that day. This will buy time now that you don't have to repay later. If students begin their pieces with clarity and purpose, they will be less likely to produce writing that requires large-scale revision later. I am not implying that writers don't discover their meaning while they write, but how students process their thinking through talk can provide at least an initial glimpse into how successful their writing will become.

Let's look at these broad topics—what to say, what to teach, and managing time—in the context of a real conference with a fifth grader.

Getting to Know One Writer: Ryan

If we are observant, we can get to know our writers even before they talk with us. One glance at Ryan's writer's notebook cover (Figure 2.1) tells me he likes baseball. It is full of baseball cards and team stickers. Flipping through a few pages of the notebook teaches me something else: Ryan is the kind of writer who does not hesitate to begin writing. He is fluent, and the titles on each page show me that he is organized as well.

Here is an excerpt of the brief conversation I had with Ryan the first day I met him. Italicized annotations address the issues of what to talk about, teaching points, and time.

Figure 2.1 Ryan's notebook cover

"Tell me what you have been working on as writer." *This is a common way to begin a conference and can be used at any stage of the writing process.*

"I was writing about when I was playing in my baseball World Series."

"Your baseball World Series—so this is something that really happened to you. Is that the kind of thing you like to write about a lot?" *I frame the dialogue as much as possible around writing, even when mentioning the writer's interests.*

"Yes. I didn't get to finish this part. Then we took different nouns and verbs and did some quick-writes. And then we wrote about a setting, and I wrote about Disney World and riding on Splash Mountain. Then we wrote about a color and mine was blue, and I wrote about the ocean when I went to California and I was playing in the ocean and stuff."

"So it sounds like you're the kind of writer who writes about what happened to you." *My talk here helps establish Ryan's identity as a writer. I am trying to be factual here—I am not saying, "You are a good writer." Rather, I am letting him in on the conversation by wondering if he agrees.*

"Yeah."

"So what are you working on right now?" *This question lets Ryan know that I have the positive assumption he has been working in his notebook.*

"Right here I was writing about last Wednesday when we had baseball practice. Some new kids are on our team—it was their first day at practice and they were nice. At the end here I wrote in italics and went back in time."

"Interesting. Why did you make that choice as a writer?"

"Putting in italics lets the reader know it's going back in time."

"Is there a writer who influenced you to make that choice? Or have you seen that in books?" *This question helps Ryan to imagine he is doing work that other writers do.*

"I've seen it in lots of different books."

"So you are the kind of writer who likes to use ideas you get from other writers."

(After reading this italicized section, I asked Ryan what he was planning to do next.)

"I was thinking of starting a fiction story."

"That's interesting. Why do you think you would like to change to fiction?"

"Because I have a lot of true stories, and I want to write something longer."

"Do you have ideas for what you might write about?"

"Not really. It's hard to think."

"Do you want some advice on how you might get some ideas?"

"Yes."

"One thing that fiction writers do is that they think about what is important to them in their real lives. Have you read the *Diary of a Wimpy Kid* books?"

"Yeah."

"Well, those stories aren't all really true, but they are based on what Jeff Kinney's life was like in middle school. He thought about what in his life had happened that might make an interesting story. Another thing that some writers do is come up with something completely different than what happened to them. Like J. K. Rowling. She wasn't a wizard, but she decided people might like reading about a boy who was a wizard. Why don't you try to generate some ideas first and I will check in with you later to see how it's going." *This is the first time I offer advice. After understanding that Ryan is a flexible writer who thinks of the work he is doing in the context of the "real world," I feel he is ready for advice about how to proceed with the fiction idea.*

"Okay."

Typically, my pattern is to provide students with a clear direction after I finish a conference. Then, I leave to meet with another writer and check back in with the first student after the second conference.

When I returned, Ryan had developed a series of ideas for fiction stories (Figure 2.2) and decided to combine his interest in baseball with his goal of trying out fiction. He decided to write about a baseball team in outer space.

Figure 2.2 Ryan's brainstorming list

My purpose for conferences early in the year is to know my students as people and as writers. As I noted with Ryan, while I was noticing that baseball was an important theme in his notebook, I also learned about him as a writer by noticing the volume of writing in his notebook and by asking him some questions. I try to use these sentence starters whenever I notice or wonder about something in order to focus on the student as writer:

"I noticed you are the kind of writer who _____."

"Why did you make this choice as a writer?"

"It seems that you are the kind of writer who . . . "

"You remind me of _____ (insert name of professional writer or other student in the class here). He/she is a writer who _____."

The Architecture of a One-on-One Conference

How do we structure the talk in a writing conference? Earlier in this chapter I provided some sentence frames to start various kinds of writing conferences. But once you start, how is a conference supposed to "go"?

I am not a fan of strict rules about what is essentially a dialogue between a teacher and a writer, but I believe there are some essential components to a one-on-one conference.

Notice the Positive

Regardless of how we enter into a conference with a student, it is essential to first mention something positive the writer is doing. As Peter Johnston points out in *Choice Words*, we must guard against looking only for deficits:

> Focusing on the positive is hardly a new idea. It is just hard to remember to do it sometimes, particularly when the child's response is nowhere near what you expected. Indeed, the more we rely on expectations and standards, the harder it is to focus on what is going well. Certainly, teaching to normative expectations will mean lots of positive feedback for some students (but not necessarily any new learning) and lots of negative feedback for others. Much more important is noticing—and helping students to notice—what they are doing well, particularly the leading edge of what is going well. (2004, 13)

Johnston's comment about some students receiving "lots of negative feedback" is powerful. In my graduate class on the teaching of writing at the University of Colorado at Denver, I often ask teachers to think for a few minutes about feedback they have received as writers. Often, more than half the teachers in the class have vivid memories of negative feedback all the way back to elementary school! The power of feedback cannot be overestimated. Remember that sincere praise is also memorable: more and more often, I hear from teachers that they did have that writing mentor who supported them with positive, rather than negative, feedback. As noted earlier, "praise" does not mean we tell students they are good writers. One of the most effective ways to be positive is to merely state what you see:

"Your words make a picture in my mind here."
"This lead makes the reader want to continue the story."
"You list three clear examples of how annoying your sister can be when she is in charge of you."

Clarify or Question

Once we notice something positive, we can make sure we understand a writer's intentions. We can ask clarifying questions or wonder about the topic before we move on to giving feedback. Here are some questions and sentence frames that may support this kind of talk:

"How do you plan to continue with this piece? What comes next?"
"I have a question about this part. I want to make sure I understand why _____."
"Tell me more about _____."

Teach

Once we have established what is going well and clarified any questions, we are ready to teach. The most important thing to remember about our teaching points is that students must be ready for our advice. If I recommend something students are not ready for, then they will probably not grow as writers. It's about setting the bar appropriately.

In the introduction, I shared my revision conference with VaShaun. I knew he was ready for advice on revision because he asked for this kind of support, and I knew the kinds of revision tools he had practiced in class.

In this chapter, I knew Ryan was ready to brainstorm some new ideas because of the volume of writing in his notebook and because of his confidence as a writer.

Knowing our writers is key to finding an effective teaching point. The kinds of questions and sentence frames I often use before deciding on a teaching point appear below:

"How can I support you?"

"Can I give you some advice about this part?"

"What do you want to work on today as a writer: _____ or _____?"

Teaching Students About Conferences

One of the keys to a successful conference is the give-and-take nature of a true dialogue. A conference should be comfortable. It should feel like a conversation. In a successful conference, the teacher and student must be speaking the same language and must understand the same terms about writing. The first steps to a successful conference, then, begin during mini-lessons as students and teachers practice the language of a successful conference together.

The key to teaching the student how to talk like a writer—how to mention specifically what he or she needs to move forward—is to teach the expectations of a conference. This can happen in several ways:

1. You can hold a conference with a student in front of the entire class and ask students to observe, noting how the conference sounds. After the model conference, you can ask students to debrief with you about what they noticed—how the teacher talked, listened, asked questions, and eventually gave advice. Students can also notice how the writer shared, responded, and listened to the suggestions given.

2. You can videotape a conference you have with a student, or show a professional video of a teacher conferring with a student.

3. You can provide an example and a nonexample of how a conference should sound. During a conference demonstration, you can ask a student to just keep repeating "I don't know" or to just talk about the topic of the piece, for example, rather than really thinking and responding like a writer. Then, you can let students know that this is a nonexample of an effective

conference because the writer is not providing enough information for the teacher to provide support.

4. You can teach the language of a conference directly to students by giving them cues to practice. For example, they might be cued to begin statements in this way:

- "As a writer I am working on _____."
- "You can support me as a writer by _____."
- "I am working on _____. My next step as a writer will be to _____."

Of all these suggestions, the most successful teaching for me has happened when I have a successful conference and ask the student to "rewind" the conference and show the class the way a conference might work.

Record-Keeping During One-on-One Conferences

One-on-one conferences are powerful. They provide opportunities to learn about writers and to assess where they are so that, together, you can develop guideposts for where they might go.

There are many ways to keep track of conferences. You might develop a recording sheet with various topics listed in anticipation of what you might discuss, and then fill in these topics as you talk with students. You might separate the two general topics to discuss with writers (their product and their processes) so that you can consider these two elements of writing as you meet with each student. I know teachers who also keep notes on paper with premade gridlines. All three of these options are provided in the appendix in the back of this book and reproduced here as Figures 2.3, 2.4, and 2.5. Whatever is used, it is important to keep track of what you talk about in a conference. I used to think I would remember the topics discussed later in the day, or I would promise myself to take notes during lunch or right after school when the conference was fresh in my mind. But, in fact, taking notes during a conference is actually the method I have found to be most useful.

NAME	IDEA	ORGANIZATION	WORD CHOICE	CONVENTIONS

Figure 2.3 Conference Notes by Category: Personal Narrative

NAME	PROCESS NOTES (HOW EFFECTIVELY STUDENT GENERATES IDEAS, DRAFTS, REVISES, AND EDITS OWN WRITING)	PRODUCT NOTES (NOTES GRADE-LEVEL EXPECTATIONS: ORGANIZATION, WORD CHOICE, GENRE-SPECIFIC REQUIREMENTS)

Figure 2.4 Conference Notes: Process and Products

Figure 2.5 Conference Record-Keeping Form: Blank Grid

Whenever I go to my doctor now, one thing that has changed is his note taking on the computer during our visit. I appreciate that he looks at me when he asks a question, then listens, and then takes notes. The note taking calms me a bit because I feel as though he is concerned enough to *get it right*. So, when I meet with students about their writing, I feel the same way. I want to *get it right*. I want to have some type of record of our conversation so that when we meet again, I can recall specifically what we talked about.

I have noticed that some students wonder why I am taking notes, so now I include in any conference with students a verbal explanation of my note-taking form: "I am going to keep track of what we talk about and the goals we set. Is that okay? I want to write notes about what you are writing about and how things are going for you as a writer. If we set goals for you, I will take notes about that too. Just let me know if you have any questions about what I am taking notes about, since this is about you!"

Regardless of the forms used for keeping notes, a few nonnegotiables might help frame what tool you choose. You can create your own list. These three ideas are just my guidelines for what I want to learn during a conference and how I hope to support my writers:

Notes should reflect the following:
- What a student is doing well in terms of process, product, or both.
- What I can teach the student about writing processes and products as they continue.
- The specific goal for the student to work on once the conference ends.

The goal is the most important item to record. If I do not actually keep track of what I teach during a conference, the danger is that I will move on to a new writer, and the student will not try to improve or work on goals. If I don't have a goal in mind to support the writer, then I am missing a key part of a conference in the first place: to teach something.

Conferring with English Language Learners

So many of us now work with English language learners in our classrooms. The same basic tips I provide throughout this chapter, regarding what to talk about, what to teach, time, and record-keeping, apply to language learners, but there are a few unique things to keep in mind.

The Writer's Level of English

I struggle the most during conferences with language learners when I fail to remember the level of English a student brings to the conference. To avoid confusion, ask many questions up front. Ask some of the same kinds of questions I recommend earlier in the chapter ("What is your piece about?" "Tell me about this part." "What are you working on today as a writer?"), and then gather all the information you can about vocabulary and syntax development before providing advice.

The Language Demands of the Genre Study

When we confer with language learners, we must keep in mind the demands of the genre they are writing. The more varied the demands, the more difficult the writing may be for the student. Ironically, personal narratives might be the most difficult genre for some of our language learners. This is due in part to the modeling you provide. For example, I often write about my cat, Milo, using detailed pictures and words when working with primary students. Language learners (and others in the class as well) often copy my ideas. Suddenly, many students have cats named Milo! But pause for a moment and think about what I have done for students. I have spent four or five minutes talking in an animated way about my silly cat, charting his adventures in pictures and words. Then, I say, "Off you go! Write your own stories!" What would you do in a similar situation if you moved to a country and you were asked to write a story in another language? Perhaps some students copy or mimic because that is exactly what they think they are supposed to do.

The issue with personal narratives is that they are personal, so by default, your stories are not your students' stories. The most successful way I have managed to confer with beginning language learners is by sticking with nouns. I ask a lot of questions about who is in the story, where they went, and, as appropriate, what they ate. Language learners who know more English can use action verbs and adjectives.

An alternative is to guide students to write about a common experience. For example, you might start your mini-lesson by saying: "We are going to be working on writing our opinions, so let's start by choosing our favorite playground equipment. Let's think about all the things we could do at recess, and then talk with a partner about what we like to do the most at recess before we write." The goal here is to frame language more narrowly during the beginning of a unit of study. I firmly believe in student choice, but when we want students to write in a new genre, we might narrow the choices a bit to collectively build some language in the genre.

Conferring with Language Learners: Two Examples

Adding Details: A Conference with Yolizma

Yolizma's first language is Spanish. At the beginning of third grade, her teachers Carrie Palmer and Katrina Shroyer were guiding students in the many ways writers might add details to their writing. Yolizma had drawn several pictures of the pool and the park during the brainstorming phase of the personal narrative unit. Her writing matched her level of English at this point. She used mainly simple sentence structures to tell where she was and what she was doing:

> I went to the pool with my mom. I went down the slide. It was fun.

She shared a similar story about the park:

I went to the park. I went down the slide. It was fun.

To support Yolizma, I met with her to learn more about the kinds of details she might add in speaking first. The transcript includes my thinking in italics:

Me: Yolizma, we have been working to add all the details we can in our stories. Which story do you want to read to me? *Even though she only had two pieces at this point, I wanted Yolizma to make the choice of which story to revise.*

Yolizma: This one. "I went to the pool with my mom. I went down the slide. It was fun."

Me: Yolizma, when you wrote this story about the slide, I can picture your face. I think you were smiling, is that right? You said you were happy.

Yolizma: Yes.

Me: I have a question for you about the slide. Was it a big slide? Or a small slide? *Often, with early language learners, a question that poses opposites combined with a visual reference can help a student add details to a story. I made a quick sketch of a big slide and a small slide on a sticky note when I asked this question.*

Yolizma: Big.

Me: When you went down the slide, did you go fast or did you go slow?

Yolizma: Fast.

Me: So let's think about how we can write that to add details to our story. How could you write that?

Yolizma: (pause) I don't know.

Me: Let's think about how it might start. What are you writing about? What was big?

Yolizma: The slide.

Me: The slide was _____.

Yolizma: The slide was big.

Me: And did you go fast or slow?

Yolizma: Fast.

Me: The slide _____.

Yolizma: The slide was big.

Me: And I went_____.

Yolizma: I went fast.

Me: Can you write that? *Now that we have established the kind of details we might add (big, fast), we can translate this into language. When she started to write, Yolizma hesitated even though we had practiced verbally. So, I drew a line for each of the first four words to get her started on the beginning of the sentence. I wrote "big" in the fourth blank line so that she could think forward to this word we had just learned.*

Me: So you are going to write a sentence using this word. What is this word again?

Yolizma: Big.

Me: How will you write it?

Yolizma: I was _____.

Me: Are you big? Or is the slide big?

Yolizma: The slide was big.

Me: Write the words. *At first, I overestimated Yolizma's knowledge of how to use words in sentences. The word blanks helped, and she more effectively completed the next sentence about the slide being fast on her own. I did ask her if the blank lines helped her to think about the words, and she said yes.*

Let the Student Take the Lead: A Conference with Azizbek

In the Stenhouse video *How Can I Support You?* (Overmeyer 2012), I work with Azizbek, a fifth-grade English language learner from Ukraine who has been in the United States for only a few months. He is working on his third personal narrative. Much of Azizbek's independent work has included making a labeled story map and a few sentences to go along with these stories. My goal for Azizbek is to help him add more details.

In this story, Azizbek tells about going to buy a car with his father. He has drawn pictures of handing money to the car dealer, getting in the car, and then the story map ends with a drawing of his house.

Once I establish the details of the story, I proceed to ask him some questions. I include a transcript of portions of the conference here to annotate where the conference was moving along, and where I confused Azizbek:

Me: I see you have the scenes drawn for your story. What's happening in your story?

Azizbek: My father buy a car. I pick the car. My father drive the car. Go home.

Me: So you and your father bought a car. You wrote about that under your pictures. Can you write that part about going home?

Azizbek: Okay. *Here, Azizbek adds the words "going home" to a picture of his house. This label work has already been completed on the earlier scenes in the story map.*

Me: Where is the car?

Azizbek: Here. *He adds a picture of the car.*

Me: How did you feel at the end of the day when you got the car?

Azizbek: This is finished.

Me: How did you feel? Were you excited? Were you happy? *Though I based my questions on the kind of work we had practiced earlier about adding feeling details, and even though Azizbek had told how he felt about his experiences in other personal narratives, my question confused him. I should have picked up on this when he said: "This is finished." In fact, had I followed his lead, I would have had him begin writing the story at that point, saying something like: "Great! Now, let's look back and see how you started other stories and then you can start writing this one." But I didn't. Note what happens as the conference proceeds.*

Me: (repeating) Were you happy or excited about the car?

Azizbek: Yeah.

Me: I can tell from your picture that you were happy. Was there anyone else here? I can see you, and your dad, and the dealer. Where was your mom?

Azizbek: Mom home. *Again, my mistake here is trying to "own" the story instead of letting Azizbek take the lead.*

Me: Oh. Your mom stayed at home. She was here (pointing to picture of home). What did she say when she saw the car? What did she do? *Azizbek is not ready for this kind of thinking about language in English, and I do not pick up on it quickly enough.*

Azizbek: Um.

Me: (mimicking what Azizbek might say or write) "So when we got home, my mom_____." What did she say? Did she smile?

Azizbek: Happy?

Me: Your mom was happy? Can you draw your mom being happy?

Eventually, I get back on track, and we continue the conference for about another minute or two. Azizbek begins writing his story with my support and then returns to his desk to work independently.

The reason I include this conference transcript is to demonstrate how important it is to let our writers take the lead. Particularly with English language learners, too many questions about the story may confuse them. We need to know what kind of language they can manage before asking clarifying questions and giving a teaching strategy.

Azizbek was confused in part because he is learning English, but he was also confused because he indicated he was finished, and then I asked where his mother was! He probably wondered why I was asking about his mom when she was not featured in this story about buying a car. I could have asked other questions for clarification (What color is the car? Is it a big car?) that would have led to more details in the writing, but instead, I ask about his mother, which increased, rather than decreased, the confusion.

The Role of Practice for the Teacher

Just as the students I work with are learning to be better writers and readers, my goal is to be a better teacher of writing. My conferences aren't perfect, but with each conference, I get better at listening and letting the student take the lead. I get better at knowing the kinds of cues that most often move writers forward. I get better at spotting what is going well, and what I can say to help writers become more independent.

Additional considerations for working with English language learners are discussed in more detail in the next chapter about guided writing conferences. The techniques suggested in that chapter can be used with students during one-on-one conferences, but the most common structure I use for scaffolding for English language learners is in small groups.

CHAPTER 3

One Teacher, Several Students: The Guided Writing Conference

Since each student in my class produces an individual piece of writing during the workshop, I used to believe that all conferences had to be one-on-one. It never dawned on me that there might be other possibilities for structuring conferences.

In other contexts, we often form small groups. In school, guided reading groups are very common, and in sports, players with similar needs or abilities are often grouped for feedback for short periods. I taught swimming lessons for a few years when I was in college, and there were times that I pulled a small group of students to review a particular skill while the rest of the students continued to practice.

A guided writing conference is similar to a guided reading conference. Students with similar needs meet in a small group for a specified need. This type of conference is beneficial as both a time-saving device and as a tool for working in collaborative groups with students. Grouping needs to be dynamic and short term. It should not lead to any kind of predictability for the students. After a mini-lesson, a group of students should not say to themselves, "Now the teacher is going to pull us together before we get to write." Guidance should not create dependence.

A guided writing conference is most beneficial when you know your writers well. Then you can make meaningful decisions about the small groups, and you can anticipate how they will function. Once a unit of study begins, for example, you may see that four to six students are still struggling with strategies discussed in a recent mini-lesson. You can then group them together to scaffold the lesson more efficiently.

You can also use a guided writing conference to raise expectations by pushing some writers further.

Time-saving tips were shared at length in the previous chapter, and a guided writing conference saves time in many ways. You have already established why you are meeting with the group; therefore, you will not be stuck for teaching ideas while students share their pieces. You also save time because each student benefits from all of your time. If I have six separate, one-on-one conferences for five minutes each, I have spent thirty minutes but only five minutes with each student. If I spend twenty minutes with a small group of six students, I have saved ten minutes from the one-on-one option and gained fifteen minutes of instruction for each student. Every student in a guided writing conference benefits from my time with the whole group if I manage my time and my talk carefully.

Reasons to Form Groups

Students can benefit from a guided writing conference during all parts of the writing process, from idea generation to final edits. As with one-on-one conferences, the kind of work you do depends on the needs of your writers. The following suggestions for pulling together a small group are based on the assumption that students are involved in a common writing genre (personal narrative, essay, research-based article, poetry, etc.). These are presented as possibilities only. Be careful about assumptions regarding small-group writing conferences: just because you know your students in one genre, do not assume they will present the same strengths and needs in another genre. A third grader I worked with recently struggled to write a personal narrative because so many of his ideas were too big to fit into a few pages, but when we moved to an essay unit, he had no problem with focusing on a single idea. Make sure that you first see how students respond to your instruction each day and how they engage in the writing process. For all writers, each day is slightly different and making assumptions about their needs before you give them a chance to write can backfire and create dependence.

Following this overview of possible purposes for meeting with small groups is a more detailed description of how these kinds of conferences might come alive in a classroom.

Early in a genre study, small groups might be convened so writers can more effectively do the following:

- Generate ideas
- Write a first draft
- Move from the talking/thinking stage to the writing stage
- Plan a complex or longer piece of writing

During initial drafting stages, small groups might be convened so writers can more effectively do the following:

- Organize or structure their thoughts in writing
- Use word choice appropriate to genre
- Elaborate and include specific details

While revising or editing, small groups might be convened so writers can more effectively do the following:

- Edit for conventions (e.g., sentence construction, punctuation, capitalization)
- Revise by adding important details, adding stronger words, deleting unnecessary details, or rearranging portions of a piece

Guided Writing Conferences Early in a Unit of Study

The following suggestions are framed by comments students might make during a workshop. The statements are based on what I often hear when I work with students who either resist writing or do not have enough strategies to feel successful.

"I Don't Know What to Write About."

It's what all teachers of writing dread the most. During a mini-lesson, we model our thinking, we encourage students to talk to a partner before they write, we check in to make sure everyone has an idea, and all seems to be going well. Students head back to their writing areas, and then it happens. Someone says, "I don't know what to write about."

Before giving some tips about how to work with a small group when this happens, my first line of defense is to be proactive. I typically end a mini-lesson with confirmation from writers that they have an idea. Sometimes I ask them to bring their writer's notebooks to the floor in the meeting area so that they can begin a fast draft of a piece, or I have them write down their idea before returning to write. Students must commit before they even return to their seats. Another technique I use is this language frame: "If you aren't sure where to start today, then _____," and I give them an idea. For example, I might say: "So if you aren't sure which idea to choose from, just circle one idea and talk to a partner about why you chose it. This may help you get started."

But sometimes, it still happens—a small group of students struggles to get started. Keep in mind that generating ideas should not take much time. The bulk of teaching during a genre study should focus on how to write in the genre, not on how to develop ideas in the genre. The advantage of working with a small group as they generate ideas is that they can support one another. It won't be all up to you to help them develop ideas.

What should you do after pulling together a group that lacks ideas? Here are some possibilities:

- Show students your writer's notebook, and add to your idea list in front of them. Think aloud while you do this and then ask them to think aloud in a similar way.
- Refer to any charting you have completed during mini-lessons and quickly review what writers do when they are stuck. You might gather students in the meeting area to have this discussion because you want the chart to be a tool they can use independently in the future.
- Talk with the group about what you notice about students who

have no trouble generating ideas. You might say, "I notice that some writers in our class categorize their lists and that helps them." Or "I notice during turn and talk that writers who have a lot of ideas jot some more things down after their partners share. I am thinking that their partners' ideas spark new ideas. Let's try that for a minute."

- Rehearse verbally, even if you asked students to turn and talk during the mini-lesson. You might nudge students to try to talk about at least five possible ideas using the language frame: "I could write about _____" and then ask them to count their ideas. If students are struggling more with fleshing out an idea once a topic is chosen, you might challenge them to talk for thirty seconds about this idea to make sure it will work as a topic.

"How Should I Start?"

Once ideas are selected, writers often struggle with how to begin writing. When we think of background knowledge or schema, the inability to begin writing may be caused by too much or too little of a "good thing." For example, students writing personal narratives may have big ideas and be overwhelmed or they may not have enough experience with how writers begin first drafts.

Strategies taught during mini-lessons can be reinforced during small-group teaching, or you may use these suggestions as unique teaching tips for students who need support during this phase of writing process.

- Suggest some leads that may jump-start the writing process, and demonstrate with your own writing how you might use one of these leads. For example, you might suggest students begin with "I'll never forget the time _____" or "I remember _____" or suggest they begin with character dialogue.
- If you have looked carefully at leads of mentor texts during a mini-lesson, then make copies of these leads for the small

group so that you can talk about them further. Limiting the number of mentor texts is key here. If students are struggling with getting started, too many options for how to begin may be less helpful than a few strong options.

- Name what you have noticed about students who start right away in your classroom. Don't identify these students by name—you want to highlight the strategy, not the writer. You might say, "I notice that writers who are able to get words on the page think first and then start their writing with the name of someone who was there and then they mention the place. So if they are thinking of a story about a water park, they might just get started by writing: 'My cousin Jimmy and I were at Water World and he wanted to go off the high dive.' Remember you can always go back and change things later, but it is important to try to get started so that you can get your piece down."

- Work together on how to begin a piece based on an experience you all share in common. For example, there may have been a recent fire drill, so you might say, "Remember yesterday when we were in the middle of science and there was a fire drill, and we all jumped because we were so focused on the experiment? And then we laughed when we were lining up? How might that story start? Let's try a few possibilities together." The purpose here is to develop flexibility by practicing with a common experience. It may be that some students actually choose to write about the suggested topic, but this is not the goal. The goal is to practice with a piece other than the one students are going to actually produce on their own.

Guided Writing Conferences During the Drafting Stages

When students are drafting, their needs differ. They have already produced some text, so these tips are based on the assumption that a small group has been pulled based on what you notice about their writing, not their lack of writing.

"I'm Done!"

If "I don't know what to write about" tops the list of what writing teachers do not want to hear, "I'm done!" is certainly a close second. Students who are quick to say, "I'm done!" may not care to write much to begin with, and they want to be "done" so they can go on to something else. These writers have yet to internalize the idea that writing is never truly finished—we can always go back and revise, or we can always start a new piece.

We have to be careful about how we interact with our students who are so quick to finish. Keep in mind that they, in fact, may feel they are done. I have many short samples of student writing that need no revision. So, we need to navigate our comments carefully here. If we just say, "But writers are never done," then we may be sending the message that we do not appreciate the effort a writer has given to a piece. The suggestions for working with small groups of writers about this issue vary according to why students may feel they are done. Some may be avoiding the writing process altogether, while others may not want to work any longer on a particular piece. As always, then, it boils down to purpose.

- If students say they are "done" early in a unit of study, start with the positive supposition that you just have not taught enough yet. View some of these writers as experts for future work rather than as writing avoiders. You might actually work with these writers to add a particular kind of detail (e.g., strong verbs, a bit of dialogue), and then use some of the samples they create in this small-group setting for your mini-lesson when you work with the entire class.

- If you are working in a school where students are used to a workshop setting, and a few students say they are done, you can pull this group together and find out what they typically do when they think they are finished. I might start a conversation this way: "What do you typically do when you feel you are finished?" or "What have you done before when you think you are finished with a piece?" Just as in one-on-one conferences, this allows me to learn about them as writers. I want to know what their experience has been in the past. If they say "We could just read" or "We can play a math game," then I can talk about how important it is to keep writing. I believe that, during writing time, we write. The minute something other than writing (e.g., a computer center) becomes a reward for those who are done, then I am lost. Students begin to associate being done as the sole goal of writing. So, first, meet with this group and ask them what they typically do and guide them from there. If, in response to the question about what they normally do, they say "We can revise" or "We can work with partners," then the next suggestion will be relevant.

- In a small group of experienced writers, you might want to brainstorm together some possibilities for what students can do when they say they are "done." There are several options you might offer (revise, start a new piece, work on a "free choice" piece, share with a partner), or, alternatively, you might ask these students what they might do if they are finished. When I offer these options, I make sure to let students know that whatever ideas they may offer, they must support stronger writing. This small group can become experts for the class, and they can actually become part of a mini-lesson in the near future as you continue the unit. You can ask them to report to the class about their options if they feel they are "done."

- Some students feel they are done partway through a unit of study because they may not have tried strategies outlined in mini-lessons. An effective strategy for this kind of small-group work is to gather students who might need to apply a specific strategy (e.g., using active verbs or including dialogue that moves a story forward) and review what you have already taught. You can have the group work with you to add to a piece you have begun while applying this strategy before asking them to try it on their own. The premise here is that students just need more time to practice. It is not necessarily a complete "re-teach" but rather a quick review followed by practice.

- If your goal is to push some writers further during a unit of study, you may gather these writers together. The drafting stages can provide you with the opportunity to nudge these writers. For example, you might teach third graders during a personal narrative unit some advanced options for using dialogue form, or you may encourage students to work in small groups with a fairly complex mentor text to see what crafts and styles they can incorporate into their own writing. I try to stay within the genre we are studying while working with students who are ready to move further. I do not want to give the impression to the class that a few students will write beyond the genre we are working with because this implies that they are "done" with this study and ready to begin another. Units typically last no longer than four weeks, so continued, but more advanced, practice within a genre is more meaningful than setting the stage for having a few write beyond the scope of the unit. If free-choice writing is an option in my classroom, then this is set up for all students when they have practiced within a genre study for the day. This is not just an option for a few. It has already been built into my workshop routines and, therefore, is not something I teach in a small group.

Guided Conferences Toward the End of a Unit of Study

Toward the end of a unit, different writers may emerge who need more support. Often, the writing process goes quite smoothly for some of our students, particularly those with a strong sense of themselves as writers. Remember that we should not assume the same writers need guided writing conferences throughout the unit. Base small groups on need only, not assumption.

"I Don't Have to Fix Anything. I Like It Just the Way It Is."

Sometimes, when students are not accustomed to revising as part of the writing process, they resist any suggestion that they may go back and improve their writing. They resist revising and editing for a variety of reasons, and so when we think about how we may work with small groups of students, we first must pinpoint why they do not revise independently.

We must first teach revision strategies during mini-lessons so that students can witness us working through our own processes. There are many wonderful resources for this kind of work, including *Reviser's Toolbox* by Barry Lane (1999), *The Revision Toolbox* by Georgia Heard (2002), and *Revision Decisions* by Jeff Anderson and Deborah Dean (2014).

After revision strategies have been taught, and some students still resist, then you may group them for these reasons. Some suggested strategies are included in each section.

- If students resist revising because they are new to the idea that revising is not rewriting, then reinforce the strategies you taught during mini-lessons, focusing on discrete goals that can be completed in a few minutes. For example, you may ask each student to change two words to make a clearer picture in the reader's mind. You can model this first with your own writing, and perhaps practice with your piece, and then give students a few minutes to make a decision about what to change in their own piece. Revising as replacing is typically where I begin with students who resist revision because they simply do not like to do it. I include sharing "before and after" samples of writing during this kind of small-group work so that they experience revision from start to finish in about fifteen minutes.

- If students lack the strategies for revision because they do not know what to revise, then I pull students with similar revision needs to do some scaffolded reteaching. I am going with the assumption here that a mini-lesson has already been taught for this strategy, and so this kind of small-group work will be quite efficient.

- When we ask students to edit for conventions and spelling, it is important to have a clear understanding of what students know and can do. Our purpose should not be for students to create perfect, error-free copies. Even professional writers have copy editors, and our students are on their own when we ask them to edit. I have begun to incorporate more demonstrations of how I self-edit in mini-lessons to determine any needs that might be met by convening small groups. Some students may not even really "see" their errors, while others may not know they have any errors because they have not yet internalized the grammar or conventions rules as they apply to their own writing. If a small group is pulled for editing purposes, a fair amount of individual conferring will be part of this work because each student will be working on his own writing. You might want to "chunk" the portion of text each student works on while self-editing during this work and monitor their progress after they complete each portion. Otherwise, you will just encourage a lot of guessing as students self-edit.

These descriptions of how to use guided writing conferences hopefully indicate how they can be used to differentiate for small-group instruction in the writing classroom. During one-on-one conferences, you are differentiating on an individual level, but a guided writing conference supports differentiation with more students at the same time.

Guided Writing Conferences and English Language Learners

Guided writing conferences are helpful to English language learners because they provide the opportunity to practice the language demands associated with writing in a particular genre. The one-on-one conference supports verbal rehearsal as well, but in a guided setting, each group member can verbalize, allowing students more opportunities to hear how a piece sounds in language first before writing.

When I pull language learners into a small group, I do so only because they demonstrate a common need as writers, not because they are English language learners. If other students in my class have a similar need, then I might pull them into the same group whether they are learning English or they are native English speakers.

Some common reasons for pulling ELLs early in the writing stages are typically for idea generation and double-checking so that students can verbalize their intentions as writers. As students move further into the writing process, I often pull ELLs who are struggling with precise word choice to convey the meaning they intend. Toward the end of the process, I may pull ELLs who share similar struggles with sentence construction and verb tenses. Whatever the case, one common feature when I pull ELLs is that I pay close attention to how I use language to advance the writers. I work hard to make sure they are clear about my teaching points, and I repeatedly ask them to verbalize their understanding prior to writing. For example, if I am helping them to use stronger verbs, we might work together as a group to generate strong verbs, and then I might ask each student to pick one of the verbs to use in the context of their own writing before they actually write. I want them to have an opportunity to practice verbally before they change their writing. Any opportunity I have to support ELLs to build their language skills as they work during writing is time well spent.

English language learners with similar writing and language needs can be grouped periodically to practice strategies other students may not need to work on. As with students who may lack certain strategies or skills the bulk of the class already has mastered, some language learners may need support not provided in a typical mini-lesson. An effective mini-lesson should always incorporate some mention of language demands required by the writing task, and the best teachers I work with always incorporate an element of partner talk before writing time starts. However, not all fifth-grade students need to practice subject-verb agreement, for example. Here are some possibilities for scaffolded guided writing instruction based on students' levels of English proficiency.

Beginning Language Learners

Early language learners benefit from scaffolded writing experiences that focus on the following.

Writing in their first language

English language learners who are literate in their first language should be encouraged to write in their native tongue. It doesn't matter if you cannot read the language. I have worked with first graders from Korea, for example, who spoke no English. During writing block, they write in their first language and share in their first language. They become part of the classroom routines right away when you allow them to write in their first language, and it shouldn't take long for them to start to label pictures and begin to use more English words in their writing.

Using pictures to represent writing

I incorporate a lot of pictures and drawing when I work with language learners. When writing narratives, for example, I draw pictures during my demonstration teaching, and they can see my story and then listen as I tell the story. I am no artist—don't worry about your artistic skills! It is more important to get a sketch on paper and then use language carefully while you tell your story. Students will understand by your voice intonations that you are sharing an experience, and they will then be able to draw their own stories. The advantage of pictures is they provide the opportunity for you to support students with label words. Pictures are nouns. When we learn a language, we focus on nouns first because they are the most concrete representations of language.

Working with carefully constructed language frames to support development of English

A series of yes/no questions may help you frame language for students as they practice their writing. For example, you might ask about the weather (Was it hot? Was it cold?), who was there (Was your mom there? Was your dad there?), or emotions (Were you happy? Were you excited?). All of these questions can be supported with pictures as well.

Once you have the answers to the yes/no questions, you can support students by framing language for them.

Intermediate English Language Learners

Students who know more English but are not yet fully proficient can benefit from guided writing groups that focus on the following.

Writing simple, and then more complex, sentences

If a group of students writes only labels and phrases, you can move them toward simple sentences in a guided setting. You can first model how to work with labels/phrases together, and then monitor each student while they practice with their own writing. If you want students who are only writing simple sentences to work in more complex structures, then you can again model and practice together before monitoring individual progress. Word banks and language frames are very helpful here.

Using more complex vocabulary

Beginning language learners typically learn nouns first and then move to vocabulary development so they can use a variety of verbs and adjectives. Many of your word-choice mini-lessons may be overwhelming to some language learners, so a guided group provides the opportunity to practice more vocabulary options. A typical reason you may pull students into a guided setting is to expand their word choices within a particular unit of study. Make sure to include visuals when possible during this work. For example, if you work with emotion words, you can provide faces that represent the emotion that matches the word. Pictures of people in certain action poses can support verb work. Pictures can provide scaffolded support for all of your students during mini-lessons, and then you can include even more practice and support for ELLs in a guided setting.

Proficient English Language Learners

Students who have begun to master English in both spoken and written forms may still need some practice native speakers do not require. Some reasons for guided groups of proficient language learners might include:

Writing complex sentences

Some proficient, and even more advanced, language learners might benefit from more practice with complex sentences. Concrete work on dependent and independent clauses (when appropriate at specific grade levels) can help students practice subject-verb agreement in the context of larger units of meaning. If a group is pulled to work on complex sentences, make sure to keep the focus narrow at first. If you use a sentence-modeling approach as recommended by Jeff Anderson (2007) in *Everyday Editing*, then this model can be replicated here with a small group. Jeff's approach works well for language learners because he suggests students examine correct sentences to mimic rather than use sentence correction exercises to learn grammar.

Using more academic and domain-specific vocabulary

Language learners in the more advanced ranges are ready to move more deeply into academic vocabulary. They are ready to work on more than the social aspects of language. In effective classroom instruction, all students should have the opportunity to practice speaking and writing using the language of the discipline. In other words, math teachers should teach the language of math, and science teachers should teach the specific language of science. During a guided writing setting, ELLs might practice applying domain-specific language to their writing as they work toward more precise representations of abstract ideas. More advanced students can access idea-driven essays and begin to see how ideas can be stated and defended in both speaking and writing.

Assessing This Type of Conference

The record-keeping forms I use for guided writing conferences are the same as those I use for one-on-one conference, but I use them differently. Since I know what I intend to discuss with students in advance of this type of conference, I typically make up a record sheet to use during and after I speak with students and have a chance to examine their writing. These records may be the same records I use for all conferences, or I may create new ones specifically for the conference.

For example, if I am working with a small group about idea generation early in a unit, then I simply write down their idea on my regular conference record sheet. But if I have given several mini-lessons on the importance of strong verbs or descriptive language in a writing piece, then I may create a separate recording sheet tracking student progress. I may actually record each word-choice change on the sheet, so I will need room for this type of record-keeping that I would not typically keep for the rest of the class. My purpose is to document how a student responded to a review of a mini-lesson. I use the record to help determine whether a student needs more support.

Troubleshooting the Guided Writing Conference

Guided writing conferences can come with some unique problems that you won't have in other types of conferences. Here are some issues to watch for, and some tips to help you overcome any difficulties.

The Conference Takes Longer Than Fifteen Minutes

If a one-on-one conference takes about four to six minutes, a guided writing conference should last about fifteen minutes. Any longer, and you run the risk of the small group losing interest. You also increase the possibility that the rest of your class is not using their time wisely during the writing block.

> ⊃*Tip:* Limit yourself to five minutes of explanation regarding what you want students to accomplish. Most guided writing conferences are meant to reinforce a skill you have taught in a mini-lesson, so the information is not brand-new. If the information is new because you are hoping to push advanced writers even further, then still try to keep your teaching point to no more than seven or eight minutes. If you are

working with writers who are ready for more advanced skills, you can use a bit more time for teaching and then you can leave them to practice independently. You might even leave the small group at the table and begin other conferences or check in briefly with table groups.

⊃ *Tip:* After the teaching point, send students back to their seats if you think they can accomplish the task on their own. This allows you more time to meet with other students while the small group begins working. You can always reconvene the group at the end of the writing block to see whether they have accomplished what you taught them, but having that break after the teaching can save time.

Students Become Dependent on the Small-Group Setting

Sometimes, if you meet with a group for several days, the students in this group may want to work only in the small-group setting. I have had this happen on several occasions. To prevent small-group dependence, consider the following tips.

⊃ *Tip:* Keep the groups very short term. Don't have groups last longer than two or three class periods. Make sure they know that, even though you are there to support them, they must always do the best they can when they are working independently.

⊃ *Tip:* Don't start small-group work until you have established a minimum of ten minutes of independent writing for every student. Try to check in with most or all of your students every day or every other day early in a unit of study. Make sure you monitor their independence level during the early stages of each unit. Assembling a group too early may result in some students believing you are always there to support them, so there is no reason to begin a piece of writing without your support.

⊃ *Tip:* Before convening any small group, even after you have established that they need to meet with you that day, let the independent writing time begin. Establish that everyone is working to the best of his or her ability and stamina prior to convening a group. If you pull too early, then you may create an environment in which students are waiting for their turn to be pulled into a small group.

CHAPTER 4

One Teacher, Many Students: Author's Chair and the Public Conference

Writing workshops often end with students sharing from an author's chair. It is a time to celebrate and share with an audience of peers. While I advocate using the author's chair periodically, as a place to celebrate a piece of writing publicly, I believe there are missed opportunities when students only share and there is no interaction. Since this book is about how talk can push writers further during a workshop, I will share some ideas about how to incorporate more talk and active listening into the sharing experience.

When students share, they should be celebrated, but since they have the opportunity to be in the spotlight, why not capitalize on the opportunity to help all writers grow? The talk during author's chair can originate from the writer, from the teacher, and/or from the peers who are listening in the room.

A teacher may frame the sharing in various ways:

"Before you share today, could you please share what you would like us to pay attention to?"

"Before you share, would you tell us where you are in the writing process? Are you just beginning this draft, or are you nearly done?"

The teacher can also frame the listening as follows:

"Listen for a strategy this writer uses that you might use in your own writing."

"As _____ reads his/her piece, please think about what
works best and be ready to share your thinking."

"Since we have been working on _____, share your
thoughts about what is going well after you hear a writer share.
Let's practice spotting those things we are all doing well, and
then after author's chair we can talk about what we can all do to
make our pieces even stronger."

Some language frames that might help listeners talk about the
writing appear below. The key to all of these cues is specificity. A
successful author's chair can be made much stronger when listeners
validate strengths, provide suggestions, and, most of all, internalize
some ideas for their own writing.

"A part of your piece that really sticks with me is where you write
(about) _____ because _____."

"I wonder if you could add more about _____.
I want to make a clearer picture in my mind about what really
happened."

"The part of your piece that really worked was when you
_____. Could you do the same thing in this
other part?"

Organizing Author's Chair

There are many ways to make author's chair part of the workshop
routine. If the writing time is going well, for example, and students are
building the stamina you have been pushing for, you might consider
beginning the next workshop time with author's chair instead of
ending the writing time early to fit in author's chair. Sharing time does
not have to be completely "public." Perhaps the simplest way to ask
students to share is to cue them to turn to a partner and share a piece
of writing or a favorite portion of a piece. If this is the method used,
then the listener can provide feedback as time allows, depending on
the purpose and the amount of time you have.

However you decide to structure the sharing of student writing, keep the purpose in mind. When I want students to celebrate their writing by sharing with their peers, for example, I often ask the listeners to say "thank you" in response to the shared piece. If I want more learning about the writing process to occur, then I incorporate one or more of the ideas listed above.

Example of a Public Conference

Sharing feedback with one writer in front of the room is not necessarily a common practice in elementary and middle school, but it is common in university-level writing classes or in adult workshops. I use the term *public conference* to mean an experience in which one writer's piece is discussed for an extended period. The role of the other writers in the room is to determine how the discussion about one person's writing can help their own.

I worked with Owen, a fifth grader who had been developing a fictional piece about a group of coyotes, to demonstrate for students how listening to a conference might help their own writing.

I began by asking students to think about something they would love to excel in: swimming, gymnastics, playing a musical instrument, skateboarding, or even a video game. Then, I asked them to picture a person who was very good at that activity. I gave the example of Missy Franklin, a Coloradoan and Olympic swimmer who had recently won several gold medals:

"Imagine that you wanted to be a great swimmer and then one day at the pool you saw Missy Franklin. And then her coach walks in and starts to give Missy advice about how to be an even better swimmer. What would you do?"

"Listen!" the students said in chorus.

"I think you would probably listen because you would want to know what someone would say to a person who was so good at what they did. Well, the same thing can happen in a writing conference. It could be that your teacher is talking to someone about his writing and you might be able to pick up some tips about writing just by listening in. Let's try it today when I confer with Owen."

Owen had been writing a fictional story about a pack of coyotes. He wanted help with his ending, so I started by asking him to paraphrase his story so that I could offer advice about the end.

"It's about a coyote who gets kicked out of a pack because he messes up a hunt and he goes on an adventure. Then he meets a coyote from the same pack that he had never met before. So they hear a howl from the pack and they rush into the territory to help the pack out." I quickly paraphrased the story back for Owen and asked him to name the coyotes and clarify any other problems in the narrative.

"In which part of the story do you need help?"

"With the ending. I can't seem to get an ending I like."

"Are you struggling with the ending because you don't know what you want to have happen, or are you struggling with how to word it?"

"I want to have the new leader be the son of the coyote to be kicked out, and I'm not sure how to fit that in. The coyote who comes back saves the pack and he gets into the pack because of that and he becomes the leader. Then five years later I want the son to be the leader and I want him to honor his father."

I then looked at the last two pages of Owen's piece while I asked the group to talk to a partner.

"Just turn and talk for a minute about the story. What is this story about? Then, talk about what Owen wants advice about."

While the group talked, I had a moment to clarify with Owen some parts of the story. When we gathered back together, I cued the students to think about where Owen needed support:

"So Rontio is the coyote who was kicked out, Lamparo is the leader, and Zent is Rontio's son. What does Owen want advice about?"

Jason said, "He needs help in the end to describe more about why the son wanted to honor his father."

"Right. So let's look at Owen's piece."

I read aloud the portion of Owen's piece where the leader turned the pack over to Rontio:

"Thank you, Lamparo. I am leaving now. I am not going to stay in your territory. I am sure you want me to leave."

"No! Stay!" insisted Lamparo. "This is not my territory and it is not my pack."

"What?"

"I am turning over the pack to you. I am not an effective leader."

"You can't be serious!"

"No Rontio you are now the leader of the pack."

"Thank you, Lamparo!"

All the coyotes yelped with glee.

Rontio showed all the coyotes where the new territory would be.

That night Zent (Rontio's son) caught a rabbit.

"Looks like you will be a good hunter when you grow up!" said Rontio.

240 moons later, Rontio's pups were all grown up. Pasha and Malo were on patrol and Zent was now leader. That night, Zent caught a deer and gave it to Rontio to thank him for saving him when he was little. He was being attacked by a bear. When Rontio died, Zent thanked him for saving him and for generations after that Rontio was remembered for his bravery.

I began by telling Owen what I noticed.

"So thank you, Owen. A couple of things I noticed about you as a writer. You make dialogue work to move a story forward. You could have just written: 'Rontio left because Lamparo wouldn't want him to be there.' But you took care of that through dialogue. You are the kind of writer who can move a story with dialogue. You also move through time quickly. Can I give you some advice about the ending?"

"Yes."

"As you work with time, you might think about how to help the reader understand that a lot of time has passed. When you use the words '240 moons' that helps us as readers to think about how coyotes and not people are your main characters. A few options you have here:

"You can separate the time change with a big space or you can use three dots in the middle of the page to show a big time change. But I am also thinking about how you could add dialogue at the end since dialogue is such a strength for you. You could have Zent actually tell the story he has told so many times to honor his father, Rontio. If you want to, this would help us to hear the story—you can add a speaking part since this is something you do so well anyway."

Owen said he would think about how to improve his ending, and then I turned to the class. "Please get out your papers and reflect for a minute about what you learned about writing by listening to this conversation I had with Owen. You were like an eavesdropper. You had the chance to listen in, and now it is your chance to think about what you learned." Here are a few samples from the student reflections. Skye wrote:

> I learned that if you are good at dialogue, you could rely on it in a story.

> I learned that you can add more space to show a big time change.

> You can rely on your strengths to make your own piece better.

English Language Learners and the Public Conference

As with any other conference, language learners can participate actively in a public conference and during author's chair, but we need to be mindful of their level of English so that the experience helps them as writers.

When I have language learners in the room during a public conference, it is helpful to use a story that may be familiar to everyone in the class. Often, during sharing time, students may have shared two or more versions of a story across the span of a unit. A piece that is familiar to start with will be easier for everyone to debrief during public conference, but it will be particularly helpful for ELLs.

Paraphrasing the piece a student wants support with may also be more intentional if there are many ELLs in the room. For example, if you have a student sharing a fairly complex story (as in Owen's wolf story described in this chapter), you may want to chart the story on the board to make sure everyone is clear about the events. You can ask students to participate in a brief retelling of the story as well, using a cloze procedure to make sure students understand what is happening before you or students provide advice.

Recently, in a third-grade classroom with many English language learners, Amara shared a piece about going to the pool with his cousin. The story began with Amara's mom saying that since there was no school, it would be a great day to go to the pool. The scene continued with a description of waiting on the couch with his teenage sister until his aunt picked them up to go to the pool.

For the retelling portion of the lesson, I quickly retold the story and left out some nouns and adjectives to make sure the story was clear before we talked about it:

"Fill in the blanks. Call out the words missing in the story when I retell it. Okay. Ready?"

I woke up and my mom said there was no
_____ today and I was excited because I

could go to the _____ instead. My sister
is a _____ and she is always texting on
her _____ and we waited on the
_____ for my _____ to pick us up.

Once we established that the story was clear, we discussed the kinds of details that supported the story.

A final scaffold you might consider for ELLs is to chart the sentence frames you want to use during a public conference. These charted speaking and listening frames are beneficial for all students, not just ELLs.

Troubleshooting the Public Conference

Certainly, a public conference like the one described in this chapter will be a rare occurrence in your classroom compared to sharing time. Sharing will happen perhaps every day, while a public conference may happen only a few times across a year.

Perhaps there can be an opportunity for every writer to have a public conference during the year. You would need to know your writers well so that you make sure that public feedback is a comfortable experience for students.

Here are some tips for thinking about how you might use the public conference:

> ⊃ **Tip:** Especially when demonstrating a public conference for the first time, select a writer who can articulate her writing process. The level of writing doesn't matter, but the ability to talk about writing is key.

> ⊃ **Tip:** Ask students first whether they are interested in having you confer with students about their work in front of others. Volunteers are more likely to be interested in this kind of conference.

⊃ *Tip:* Wait to use the public conference until you know your writers can generalize the feedback from the conference to their own writing. If students are struggling to implement your feedback in one-on-one or peer conferences, then you may want to wait a bit before trying a public conference.

⊃ *Tip:* To engage students more fully in the conference, you can begin by noticing something positive and then providing advice. Then you can ask peer partnerships to talk to each other in the same way about their writing. You can also ask some students to share their own praise, wonderings, and advice, which will set the stage nicely for the topic of the next chapter: peer conferences.

PART 2

Student-Student Talk

CHAPTER 5

Two Students:
The Peer Conference

Peer conferences are helpful to both teachers and students. Student writers can get valuable feedback from peers, and all of the hard work of conferring does not need to rely solely on the teacher. The peer conference is set up in a similar way to a teacher-student one-on-one conference, but there are some distinct differences to keep in mind when asking students to confer with one another.

Setting the Stage for Successful Peer Conferences

As with a small guided-writing conference led by the teacher, one of the necessary elements of a successful peer conference is an understanding of what is supposed to occur. The best way to teach this is to model. As you work with students early in the year, you can begin to determine who successfully shares ideas with peers during author's chair or peer conferences. These are the types of students—the listeners and the advice givers—it may be most logical to put together prior to asking all students to engage in a peer conference. These students can become the model for a fishbowl while other students observe. The observers can take notes about how to successfully engage in a conversation about another student's writing.

An alternative to using pairs of students as models prior to introducing peer conferences to the entire class is to actually teach students about peer conferring up front. I have tried this many times. The lesson takes a while, but here is how it went for me recently in a fourth-grade classroom at Sandburg Elementary in Littleton, Colorado. I began by explaining that writers in the "real world" seek support from other writers: "Sometimes writers get advice from teachers just like you do, but sometimes they get advice from their friends or peers. Anyone your age is your peer. Your teachers and I are a little bit older than you, so we can't be your peers."

I then took a bit of time to clarify what the topic of a peer conference might be. I explained that even though I wasn't a peer, I wanted to take a minute to talk with someone about a piece of writing they were excited about and wanted to share.

Joanna indicated she was excited about a fantasy story she was writing.

"Fantasy!" I commented. "Wow. That's a lot of work. I would love to know how you get your ideas for writing fantasy stories."

Joanna discussed how her reading influenced her writing. She liked writing the kinds of stories she liked to read.

Once she said this, I started a list.

"So, writers, one of the things we can talk about with our writer friends is how they come up with ideas." I wrote "What we can talk about" at the top of a paper under the document camera and asked the students to talk to a partner about what else they might talk about.

"So one thing you do as a writer is you come up with ideas. Think about the other work you do as a writer. What might you talk about?"

Since the students had been studying fiction as a genre, the list expanded to include many components of writing fictional narratives:

Story map
Characters
Setting
Problem
Action

Then, to get students ready for peer conferring, I gave them a tip I had learned from attending writing workshop classes at Lighthouse Writers Workshop: "When writers ask someone for advice, they usually don't ask a friend to just read it because the friend will probably just say, 'It's great' or 'It's fine' and that doesn't help. Writers ask for specific advice. So when you have a chance to talk to a peer today, you are going to be in charge. You get to decide what you want advice about. Think for a minute about what you might ask for advice on when you think of your story. Raise your hand if you might ask for advice on your ideas or on your characters."

I continued through the list, asking students to consider what they might ask for advice on.

At this point, I decided to let students try to talk with peers while I searched for a partnership that seemed to be going well. I was looking for students who were having an authentic conversation. I decided not to model a peer conference because I am not a peer. I wanted the first peer conference to actually sound like fourth graders talking.

Ethan and Zoe fit the bill. I asked them to demonstrate for the class the kind of conversation they were having. Zoe needed advice from Ethan about the sequence of events she was writing in her narrative (Figure 5.1). Here is the transcript of their peer conference:

"I need help with making my lead longer and more specific. The story is about my mom's surprise birthday party."

I cued Zoe to read her lead aloud.

"One day I was with my mom. 'My birthday is coming up' she reminded me.

Then it kind of just goes right into the story."

Ethan thought for a minute.

"Can you describe where you are with your mom? And maybe you can tell what day it is if you can remember. Maybe you can add more dialogue up here too."

I paused them for a moment to support the class in understanding how a writer can internalize advice.

"Zoe, he gave you three pieces of advice. Take a second and write notes about this advice on your form."

> Suprise! (draft 1)
>
> ~~* One day I was with~~
>
> ~~my mom.~~ "My birthdays coming
>
> up!" she reminded me.
>
> "Is the family coming over?"
>
> "NO," she responded. "I dont
>
> need a party." But since I
>
> was seven I thought that was
>
> to1taly wrong. That moment
>
> I knew I was going to plan
>
> my mom a surpise party, so
>
> I got to work! Early the
>
> next morning I snuch into
>
> her room and stole her phone.

Figure 5.1 Zoe's narrative

I then asked the class to talk with a partner about Ethan's advice. I was modeling the importance of listening to a partner. We reviewed Ethan's advice. I pointed out that anyone in the room might have provided different advice, but the point was for Zoe to think about what she might do as a writer based on what Ethan said.

We quickly charted what we noticed about the conference and labeled it "A Successful Peer Conference."

The writer

Asks for specific advice
Shows the listener a copy of the piece
Reads the piece aloud
Takes notes on the advice given

The listener

Listens first
Asks clarifying questions
Gives specific advice and uses words like this to start sentences:
  "You might _____" "Maybe you could _____"
  "I wonder if _____"

Establishing Outcomes for the Peer Conferences

The peer conference has two outcomes. Student writers will listen to and perhaps incorporate advice from peer writers, and they will also gain in their understanding of how to improve their own writing by providing advice to others. An additional outcome might include a short reflection on how the peer conference supported each writer. The point of the conference is to learn as much from giving advice as receiving it. See reflection forms in Figures 5.2 and 5.3.

Peer Conferences Versus Teacher-Led Conferences

The routines of a peer conference can match those of a teacher-student conference: the reader/listener can begin by praising the writer for something specifically accomplished, followed by suggestions. It is perhaps best to think of these offerings as "suggestions" rather than

---

Writing Workshop Peer Conference Form

My Name _____

1. My partner's name:

2. I want my partner to support me as a writer by helping me with:

3. Notes about my writing after my conference:

    Something my peer partner thought I did well:

    I could . . .

    I might try . . .

Figure 5.2 Peer conference forms for writer sharing a piece with peers

"teaching points" because successful peer conferences require the writer to make final decisions about what to add, to delete, or to change based on peer suggestions. In a teacher-student conference, it is more likely that a teacher will actually require a writer to try something to improve the writing because the teacher's role includes helping the student to become a more flexible writer. In a peer conference, however, the writer has to make the final decision about what advice to take and what changes, if any, to make.

Writing Workshop Peer Conference Form

My name ___Zoe 🖤_____

1. My partner's name:

   Ethan

2. I want my partner to support me as a writer by helping me with:
   — Making my lead bigger and more spasific
   — my story is about my moms suprise party
   — title: Suprise!

3. Notes about my writing after my conference:

   Something my peer partner thought I did well:

   I could.... Put, where, Day

   I might try... More dialogue

Figure 5.3 Zoe's peer conference form

Peers might be more successful at asking questions of one another rather than giving advice, especially early in a peer-conferring experience. After a writer shares, the reader might ask a few clarifying questions that can then nudge the writer to think of more details to add. I find that peers have more authentic wonderings because they experience the world in the same way as their peers. They might ask better clarifying questions than an adult because they have less experience with filling in the blanks of a slightly confusing narrative.

Another way to increase the success of a peer conference is to ask the writer to state on a sticky note where support is needed. If a writer sets the agenda for the conference, this writer is more likely to receive helpful advice from the peer reader.

Content Versus Grammar and Mechanics

One key to successful peer conferences is to ask students to focus on content rather than on *conventions*. All writers in your classroom have the advantage of having lived as long as other peers in your class. They have similar life experiences in the sense that fourth graders see the world through fourth-grade eyes, not through adult eyes. When the focus remains on content and not on conventions, I no longer have to worry about grouping a "strong" writer with a "struggling" writer. These kinds of labels limit expectations for writers, but they can cause particular harm in a peer conference. When setting up peer conferences, I am careful about grouping students together for the purposes of supporting one another but not based on my assumptions about the level of their writing. Remember what Carl Anderson (2000) says about writing conferences: they provide an opportunity for conversation. I firmly believe that all of my students can engage in meaningful conversations about their work if the focus is on content.

The biggest danger in allowing peers to provide advice on conventions is that students will tend to take their friend's advice, even if it is wrong. A peer may unknowingly "help" a fellow writer by correcting a mistake that wasn't an error to begin with. Editing for conventions is the work of the writer, with the support of the teacher, but not the work of other peers.

One of the rules of a peer conference is that the writer must make the changes—the writer holds the pen, not the reader/listener. If the reader takes the pen, then the purpose of the peer conference (to learn to become a better writer) is lost.

Organizing and Peer Conferences

Partnerships can be fluid or static. Some students may work best with specific peers, and other students may not mind working with anyone who is available. There is no right or wrong answer to the question of how peers should be paired, but it is important to make sure that the decision supports successful conferences. I work with some teachers who specify partners, and others who ask students to seek out someone who is available. Both approaches are successful because there are rituals and routines to support these pairings.

There are many methods for organizing and managing peer conferences. Here are a few possibilities:

- Ask students to sign up for a peer conference and to meet in a specified area of the classroom. You might have a timer in this space so that the peer conference lasts no longer than five minutes. Prior to having a conference, the writer can share with you why they want to meet with a peer.
- Choose one day every week or every other week for peer conferring. Creating a time and space for this can help you avoid the prospect of students spending more time conferring than writing.
- Allow students to opt out of peer conferring if they are not ready to share a piece. If this is an option you allow, you can still ask these students to be active listeners and readers of another student's work. Remember that when students give advice, they are still learning about writing.

Assessing Peer Conferences

The goal of a peer conference, as in all conferences, is to support writers. Avoid making record-keeping so complicated that you can't easily see whether the writing has improved. If you ask students to engage in peer conferences at the same time, then you can sit in on some conferences and monitor progress in real time. You can also provide a quick piece of advice for a reader who is struggling with how to give advice or ask questions.

If you use peer conferences on a regular basis, build a time in your workshop to check in to make sure the peer conferences are helpful tools for improving writing. Ask students in a debrief to share their thoughts about peer conferences. You can perhaps make a chart with two headings:

Peer conferences are helpful when _____

Peer conferences would be more helpful if _____

This conversation is important if you want peer conferences to continue to be successful in your classroom.

English Language Learners and Peer Conferences

English language learners can successfully engage in peer conferences. The most important factor in their success is framing the language and the vocabulary needed for this kind of conference to be successful. It might be necessary to ask students to write on their recording sheets in more detail about the advice they need, and you may need to be more careful about how you pair ELLs for a peer conference. Certainly, a beginning language learner would not find much success with a peer who speaks a different native language but is nearly proficient in English. You might also consider the genre for this kind of conference with ELLs. A personal narrative would be much more difficult in a conference setting when compared to an inform/explain piece based on a content the entire class had studied.

When I have many ELLs in a classroom, I often ask students to engage in peer conferences at the same time so that I can manage the room and listen in on as many conferences as possible. The key to any successful conference is practice, so with ELLs, you may need to practice for a bit longer.

An option for students who are less proficient in English is to create triads so that the beginning English learner can be part of the process of a peer conference. They will understand that peers are commenting on one another's writing, and as they learn more English, they can participate in this kind of talk as well.

Troubleshooting the Peer Conference

Once you have modeled for students how a peer conference might look and sound and rituals and routines have been established, you can set peer conferences in motion. Things can still go wrong. In categories, here are some tips for getting peer conferences back on track.

If students disrupt the writing during a peer conference, consider taking these steps:

- Dedicate a specific space in the room for peer conferring that is easy for you to monitor.
- Require the use of a timer so that the conference is more focused.
- Consider partnerships. If some partnerships do not work well, then reassign them as needed.
- Dedicate a set time for all peer conferences to occur so that the conferences do not happen while others are writing.
- Bring students into the conversation about disruptive behavior during peer conferences. I believe in being honest with students when disruption occurs. They are kids. My expectations are not unrealistic, but I do fully expect that, once routines are set and students can work on their independent level, students will engage in meaningful work during writing time. So when disruption prevents meaningful work, I start a conversation by saying, "Today during peer conference work, it was hard for many of us to get our work done. Let's talk about what we can do to make it better next time." We either review a chart we have already discussed about expectations during peer conference, or we create a new chart as a reference for future work.

If students' record-keeping forms during peer conferences do not provide you with enough information to know whether they are helpful, consider taking these steps:

- Ask students to debrief with you verbally right after a peer conference. You can check in to make sure the conference was meaningful.
- Show models of recording forms from students that demonstrate the success of the peer conference.
- Talk with students openly about how peer conferences are working, or not working, and ask them to help you think of ways to increase their accountability during peer conferences.

If writers during peer conferences feel criticized rather than supported, consider taking these steps:

- Clarify the purpose of the peer conference during a mini-lesson, and demonstrate clearly the difference between criticism and feedback.
- Require that peer conferences be held only when a writer requests a conference and then only for a specific purpose.
- Ask each writer who requests a peer conference to write the reason for the meeting on a sticky note. Check in with the reader of the peer conference before the conference occurs to make sure the request is clear.

Final Thoughts About Peer Conferences

Remember that peer conferences provide a structure that can support your writers, but in the end, the goal is to make sure that talk in the writing workshop supports as many writers as possible. Some years, peer conferring supports all writers in my classroom, while in other years, I struggle either because of personality conflicts or because of difficulty with steering students away from focusing only on mechanics when looking at their peers' work. When it isn't going well after peer conferring has been discussed and taught, I do not require all students to engage in peer conferences.

A more helpful structure for peer feedback, in my experience, is found in the peer review conference, the focus of the next chapter.

CHAPTER 6

Several Students:
The Peer Review Conference

I have participated in many writing conferences, retreats, and workshops as an adult. One of the main differences between these opportunities to learn from professional writers and peers and my experiences as a teacher is the amount of talk. In adult, "real-world" workshop settings, we all talk. A lot. And we rarely, if ever, confer one-on-one with the workshop leader.

I had the opportunity to study with Mark Doty, the National Book Award–winning poet and memoirist, at the Port Townsend Writers' Conference in Washington State. For six days, fourteen budding poets sat around a table and read one another's poems, listened as Doty provided specific advice to two poets a day, and talked about our goals and ideas. I spent about twenty hours around the table that week, and only thirty minutes was devoted to my own work. But the other nineteen hours and thirty minutes of talk helped me even though it wasn't all directed at my own poetry.

The talk was purposely framed to help all of us. Doty made sure that, as we commented on one another's work, we provided specific responses, and he interrupted often and used phrases such as:

"So if you are trying to write a poem like this, you might
    consider _____."
"One thing I am learning about you as a poet is that you
    tend to _____."
"An author you might want to read is _____."

If someone had alerted me in advance that I would only have the opportunity to hear comments on my poems for about thirty minutes in the six-day workshop, I honestly do not know whether I would have attended. But because of Doty's facilitation skills, I was able to learn as much, if not more, from the discussions of others' works as I was my own. This is probably due in part to the lack of emotion surrounding comments about someone else's writing. Writers are naturally more connected to what they write because they experience the process and know exactly what they "mean"; yet, when we read others' works and listen to comments about another person's writing, the emotion is removed because we are not personally involved.

I wanted to see whether this type of peer review structure would work in a school setting. One of the differences in working with adults is that you can count on them to have read pieces carefully in advance. No one in my workshop with Mark Doty was uninterested. Otherwise, they would not have paid the fee and given up a precious summer week if they were not going to be engaged in talks about writing! So, how best to ensure complete engagement, about both writing and self-reflection, in a typical classroom setting?

Setting the Stage for Successful Peer Review Conferences

Once students are familiar with one-on-one peer conferences, they will have practiced the language of the peer review conference already. They will know how to give effective feedback and how to focus on content rather than on grammar and mechanics.

To get students ready for a peer review conference, I often refer to my conferences with them, and their conferences with one another: "You know how I sometimes give you feedback on your writing, and then sometimes you give feedback to each other? Well, that's one way that we can all become better writers. Another way is to do this same kind of work in a small group. That's what happens when I take writing workshops: we talk in a small group about each other's writing."

Organizing and Managing Peer Review Conferences

Limit the number of students in the peer review conference to four or at most five. Depending on your group dynamics, you may want to spend a bit of time thinking about how to form groupings. I have found that a range of writers in each group is most supportive for this kind of work.

This kind of conference has been most successful for me when a genre study has generated enthusiasm and students are in the midst of fairly strong drafts. You want to make sure each student shares at least half to a full page of writing, and you also want to make sure students do not share five or six pages. Limiting the amount of text per writer, while making sure that everyone has at least some writing to share, is key. If you try this too early in the drafting process, then the only feedback a writer might receive is to write more.

The best way to make sure students read work in advance for this type of conference is to provide everyone in the group with a copy of the writer's work. Students can share their work on a secure blog or website set up at the school, or, alternatively, the teacher can make copies. Once everyone has a copy, a decision has to be made: Will the writer lead the conference, or will the readers begin without the writer speaking at all? There are benefits to both. It depends on the purpose of the conference, and it may be up to the writer.

If the writer leads the conference, then it is best for the writer to set the stage for the meeting. For example, a writer may need support on a lead or on an ending to a story. A writer may not think one part is completely clear and therefore may need support to make sure meaning is being made.

If the readers lead the conference, then it is best if someone starts the conversation with a noticing or praise: "Mark is writing about his first experience on a roller coaster, and I noticed that he is trying to really build up the moment before the ride happens." Or, someone can offer up a question: "I wonder if Mark wants the reader to picture the ride itself or to feel the fear before the ride?"

The typical rules about one-on-one conferences must apply here. The intent is to support and provide meaningful feedback to the writer, not to criticize. Comments and questions should all be made with the intention of supporting the writer, not co-opting the writing with our own ideas.

The peer review conference is most effective when it seems relatively "new" each time you ask students to engage in this type of work. Peers should speak frequently with one another about their writing, but the formality of a peer review conference implies that the student has a real need that can best be met by meeting with a group of peers. Peer conferences are most suited for personal narrative and fictional narrative because these genres require a strong sense of making meaning. All writers in the group, since they are the same age, can support their peers as they seek to make meaning in narrative genres. If the writing doesn't make sense, it will be easy for peers to ask questions to support the writer. Research-based writing may be a bit more complicated to apply to this conferring format because a certain amount of background knowledge may be needed to support peers when they are engaged in research.

Preparation is key. Before the conference, make copies of students' work and inform students of their group assignments. Then, when the peer group meets, students are ready to support one another.

The rules listed below were set up in advance of the peer review conferences to promote efficiency. This is the sequential procedure (protocol) we followed:

Writer hands out copies and thanks listeners.

Writer paraphrases the piece if it is unfamiliar to the group: "My piece is about _____."

Writer seeks advice: "I need help with _____."

Writer reads section aloud and repeats need for advice.

Listeners ask clarifying questions as needed.

Listeners talk with one another about the piece while writer takes notes.

Writer thanks group members and makes a plan for next steps.

Listeners consider what they learned about writing in the specific
genre because of the discussion.

Records of one peer review conference with a group of four students
can be found in this chapter.

Ashley, Owen, Kody, and Jaden were in the midst of a fictional
narrative unit. They set the stage prior to the conference by asking for
specific kinds of help for their stories. During the conference, each
writer took notes about what he or she might revise after the round of
conferences was complete, and after each session, the other writers in
the group took notes about what they learned from each conference.

Let's look at Ashley's record sheet (Figure 6.1) to examine a record
of the conference. Ashley's piece is about a girl who wants a puppy.
She was working on a scene about going to the pet store, and she
wanted support about specific kinds of smelling details she might use.

Ashley's group easily supported her with some ideas after she read
her piece aloud:

"You could add like the smell of the dog's fur," suggested Kody.
"Or even that it smells like dog poop!" said Owen.
The group laughed.
Owen defended himself: "It does smell like dog poop sometimes
though."
Ashley recorded the ideas that resonated for her:
Say it smelled like dog fur. Add periods. Fresh dog doo doo.

Ashley was an active contributor to conversations about the rest
of the group's writing as well. She recorded what she learned from
discussions about stories by Jaden, Kody, and Owen (Figure 6.2).
Reflecting on what we can learn while discussing other writers' work
is tricky, but Ashley is an example of someone who understands
this process. She was able to generalize the comments and therefore,
potentially, apply these strategies or crafts to her own writing (see
Figure 6.3).

Writing Workshop Peer Review Conference Form

My name __Ashley__

1. My partners' names:
   Oven
   Kody
   Jaden

2. I want my partners to support me as a writer by helping me with:
   using descriptions by using the smell

3. Notes about my writing after my conference:

   Something my peer partners thought I did well:

   I could.... say it smelled like dogs fur, Add Periods, Fresh dog stuff doo doo

   I might try...

Figure 6.1 Page 1 of Ashley's peer review conference form

Kody is another writer from Ashley's group. As preparation for his piece about Martians invading Earth, he was very general in his request from his partners (Figure 6.4): "I need help seeing if page 5 of my story is good or not. Or if I need to add anything." Even though this is not a very specific request, Kody did take quality notes about advice he received. When I look at his form, I see that he may go back and add more about details about the Martians and the disguises they wear as they plan to invade Earth. His notes from what he learned from

Something I learned when we talked about __Jaden__'s writing:

use commas to slow down the moment
Use action to make the scene faster

Something I learned when we talked about __Kody__'s writing:

Could use fantasy
Titles for differnt Ex. Aliens
charactors
People

Something I learned when we talked about __Owen__'s writing:

Use lots of descriptions

Something I learned when we talked about _____'s writing:

Figure 6.2 Page 2 of Ashley's peer review conference form

other peers' conferences contain some specificity as well (Figure 6.5): He learned from talking about Jaden's piece that a writer can speed up and slow down the moment, and he learned from discussions about Ashley's piece that one way to describe is to add sensory details. Kody's notes prove that a peer review conference can strengthen students' revisions while discussing their own pieces (see Figure 6.6) and while talking about the pieces of other writers in their small group.

Pg. 2   Ashley

closer. "PLEASE,"
   "Only if you don't ask to
buy a dog. Promise?"
   "Promise,"
  "Calvin we have to go."
  "I was in the middle of my
video game," Calvin grumbled.

I jumped into my moms honda car
and we sped up to Puppys n'
stuff I jumped out and
walked into the place. How
awful it smelled in here
you had to get used to
it I got used to it
and went in. How cute they
were small and some mediam

Figure 6.3 Ashley's writing shared during peer review conference

Writing Workshop Peer Review Conference Form

My name **Kody**

1. My partners' names:

Jaden
Owen
Ashley

2. I want my partners to support me as a writer by helping me with:

I need help with seeing if pg. 5 of my story is good or not. Or if I need to add anything

3. Notes about my writing after my conference:

Something my peer partners thought I did well:

I could.... what kind of disaisue
More discripdive
what planet
what Marshen is

I might try...

what kind of disaisue
More discripdive
what planet
what Marshen is

Figure 6.4 Page 1 of Kody's peer review conference form

Something I learned when we talked about _Jaden_'s writing:

is that you can speed up and slow down the , moment.

Something I learned when we talked about _Owen_'s writing:

Description is imortant

Something I learned when we talked about _Ashley_'s writing:

you could use your 5 senses.

Something I learned when we talked about _____'s writing:

Figure 6.5 Page 2 of Kody's peer review conference form

pg5   Draft 1

                Kody
know you are here!"

            Marshens

"Should we come out?"asked Savager.

"No,"said Captain Atten. They waited

until the humans left and ran in.

    "Should we get a discise on?" asked

Jock.

    "Yes we should," answered Comander

Code. When they got suited up they went

to the training room to practice.

            Humans

"Lets leave,"said Jade "It's getting

late." So they left and went to the

training room. They practiced every thing they did

Figure 6.6 Kody's piece of writing shared during a peer review conference

Peer Review Conferences Versus Other Structures

As mentioned earlier, I recommend the peer review conference much less frequently than the more common one-on-one structures found in daily conferences. But the uniqueness of the peer review conference has benefits, and certainly, the knowledge that three or four other writers will be critiquing your work can raise the bar and the enthusiasm in the group for writing. When I have experienced these kinds of conferences for my own writing, I have been nervous, almost dreading the moment when my work is shared and critiqued. My experience with young writers is that this is not the case. Perhaps they have not been jaded by the feeling that they will only be criticized by other writers. In fact, the level of engagement every time I have used peer review conferences in grades three through seven has been extremely high. Even resistant writers have been fully engaged when they are talking about their writing and listening to advice from a small group of peers.

Assessing the Peer Review Conference

The record-keeping form I include in this chapter (Figure 6.7) is meant as a suggestion. From having experimented with peer review conferences for many years now, I have moved to this more edited form. The goal is to promote talk that supports writing and not to require a lot more reflective writing. This form can be filled out in a few minutes and is meant to be used during and right after the peer reviews.

Writing Workshop Peer Conference Form

My Name _____

1. My partner's name:

2. I want my partner to support me as a writer by helping me with:

3. Notes about my writing after my conference:

   Something my peer partner thought I did well:

   I could . . .

   I might try . . .

Figure 6.7a Page 1 of peer review conference form

Something I learned when we talked about _____'s writing:

Something I learned when we talked about _____'s writing:

Something I learned when we talked about _____'s writing:

Something I learned when we talked about _____'s writing:

Figure 6.7b Page 2 of peer review conference form

When I read over these records, I am mainly looking for specificity. When I look at Ashley's, her specific references to what she could do help me know she listened to her group. In her reflections about what she learned while discussing the writing of other group members, I also note the specificity. She notes, for example, that fantasy writers might use titles to separate the scenes with different characters. She is not quite as specific with her reflections on Owen's writing ("use lots of descriptions"), but I remind myself that these students are ten years old, and they are only beginning to work with the idea that writers can benefit from talking with other writers. The goal of this kind of record-keeping is to get a status of the class to determine how peer conferences are working.

My best assessment of this kind of work comes when I debrief with the entire class at the end of a peer review session. We meet together on the floor and discuss how things went. I open with a discussion starter: "So writers, today we tried a peer review conference and it's time to think about if this was helpful. If it was, let's be specific about why it helped you as a writer. If it was not helpful, let's talk about how we can make the experience more helpful without pointing out anyone in our group. For example, if you feel a person in your group did not provide helpful feedback, or a group member was not really paying attention, don't say the person's name or be negative in any way. Say something like this: 'It would be more helpful if every group member gave me some advice about my writing instead of just one person.'"

My goal is to make peer review conferences successful because I have seen them work well for many years. I do not abandon them, which is why I recommend to students that we talk about what makes them work rather than deciding whether to use them.

Peer Review Conferences and ELLs

My advice for using peer review conferences with English language learners is similar to the advice for peer conferences. Language frames may need to be more intentional, though I did include some possibilities in the suggested record-keeping form.

I would not recommend placing all ELLs together unless there is a compelling reason for this. For example, you might have a small group of students who write in their own language and speak very little English. Perhaps these students could be grouped for a short time for a peer review conference.

Even if a student speaks very little English and has very little writing completed, the *process* of being part of a peer review conference is powerful. If the student does not have enough language to ask for specific kinds of support, then perhaps you can sit with this group when it is time for the language learner to share her writing. You can guide the group to say something positive about the writing, pointing to the page, and encouraging the writer to keep going. I would hesitate to exempt the language learner from the opportunity to be a part of this work. Even if, as a teacher, you read the piece aloud to the group and everyone smiles and supports the writer through verbal praise, then the message is that everyone is part of the group and the purpose is not to criticize.

Troubleshooting the Peer Review Conference

This kind of conference can be tricky. Here are a few tips to help them go more smoothly.

If you feel you will run out of time for a peer review conference:

- Explain the entire procedure at the end of one writing period, and then provide an entire forty-five-minute block to the review process the next day.
- Make sure you have copies of every student's paper in folders that can be handed out to the groups so that your problem isn't paper and materials driven.
- Set a timer. About seven to ten minutes per person should be enough time to discuss the writing. Remember that an excerpt of the writing can be discussed. If a story is long, a few paragraphs or one page can be plenty to discuss.

If students are not on task during the peer review conference:

- Do a quick "check-in" after each timed conference. Name what is going well ("I noticed how specific you are trying to be about the writing."). Name what you would like to see changed ("I noticed some of you are going right to conventions. Remember you need to give feedback about the content based on what the writer wants to know.").
- Assign a moderator for each group who will ask each group member to contribute to the discussion.
- Use a "fishbowl" method by asking the entire class to watch one successful group's peer review conference. A discussion about what makes a peer review conference work can be held after the fishbowl.
- In advance of the first "whole-group" peer review conference experience, tape a successful group holding a peer review conference. Show this video to the class as a way of providing a model of what you expect.

CONCLUSION

One final story about how talk transformed one writer in my fifth-grade classroom. About twelve years ago, I taught a student named Carrie, who had some difficulties with writing. She had an individualized education plan (IEP) for writing, but she improved tremendously during her fifth-grade year.

One day during a poetry study, I noticed that Carrie had used imagery in her poem about the ocean. I used her piece as an example of what I meant by imagery.

Fast-forward ten years. Carrie was a student at the University of Arizona. She contacted her mother, a friend of mine and a teacher in my district, so that she could e-mail me about the memory of that day when I used her poem. Here is Carrie's e-mail:

> Hi Mr. O,
>
> I got your email from my mom, I hope that's ok. I'm taking a non fiction writing class this semester today in class we talked about our first real experience being writers. I talked about when you taught the class about imagery. I wrote about the first time I saw the ocean and you used my poem as an example, I thought I was so cool. You were one of the teachers I had that never made me feel dumb for having an IEP. I'm so lucky to

have had you as a teacher. I hope that everything is going well in your life!

Sincerely,

Carrie

Sent from my iPhone

I was stunned. As a college student, Carrie remembered a tiny moment during a fifth-grade writing workshop. But in the context of the topic of this book, it seems appropriate to share a story about the power of talk. My class discussed how Carrie used imagery ten years ago. From what I recall, it was a short discussion, and her piece was one of several samples I shared that day.

A specific, public comment about her writing created a permanent memory for Carrie. Most important, it created a *positive* memory. That's what we have the power to do every day as teachers of writing: create a positive memory about what it is like to be in a community of writers.

I do not share Carrie's story to pat myself on the back. I share it to thank you—all of the writing teachers–who make a difference in the lives of children every day. Keep them writing, keep them talking, and create positive stories for you and for them every day.

Off you go.

APPENDIX

Conference Notes
and Record-Keeping Forms

Conference Notes by Category: Personal Narrative

NAME	IDEA	ORGANIZATION	WORD CHOICE	CONVENTIONS

Let's Talk: One-on-One, Peer, and Small-Group Writing Conferences by Mark Overmeyer.
Copyright © 2015. Stenhouse Publishers.

Conference Notes: Process and Products

NAME	PROCESS NOTES (HOW EFFECTIVELY STUDENT GENERATES IDEAS, DRAFTS, REVISES, AND EDITS OWN WRITING)	PRODUCT NOTES (NOTES GRADE-LEVEL EXPECTATIONS: ORGANIZATION, WORD CHOICE, GENRE-SPECIFIC REQUIREMENTS)

Let's Talk: One-on-One, Peer, and Small-Group Writing Conferences **by Mark Overmeyer.**
Copyright © 2015. Stenhouse Publishers.

Conference Record-Keeping Form: Blank Grid

REFERENCES

Anderson, Carl. 2000. *How's It Going? A Practical Guide to Conferring with Student Writers.* Portsmouth, NH: Heinemann.

Anderson, Jeff. 2007. *Everyday Editing: Inviting Students to Develop Skill and Craft in Writer's Workshop.* Portland, ME: Stenhouse.

Anderson, Jeff, and Deborah Dean. 2014. *Revision Decisions: Talking Through Sentences and Beyond.* Portland, ME: Stenhouse.

Dweck, Carol. 2006. *Mindset: The New Psychology of Success.* New York: Ballantine Books.

Graves, Donald. 1984. *Writing: Teachers & Children at Work.* Portsmouth, NH: Heinemann.

Hattie, John. 2011. *Visible Learning for Teachers: Maximizing Impact on Learning.* New York: Routledge.

Heard, Georgia. 2002. *The Revision Toolbox: Teaching Techniques That Work.* Portsmouth, NH: Heinemann.

Johnston, Peter. 2004. *Choice Words: How Our Language Affects Children's Learning.* Portland, ME: Stenhouse.

Lane, Barry. 1999. *Reviser's Toolbox.* Shoreham, VT: Discover Writing.

Overmeyer, Mark. 2012. *How Can I Support You?* (DVD). Portland, ME: Stenhouse.

Tovani, Cris. 2012. "Feedback Is a Two-Way Street." *Educational Leadership* 70 (1): 48–51.

Wiggins, Grant. 2012. "Seven Keys to Effective Feedback." *Educational Leadership* 70 (1): 10–16.